LINUX Administration

kernel version 2.0 to 2.2

All trademarks quoted are the property of their respective editors.

All rights reserved. No part of this publication may be reproduced, stored in a retrieval system, or transmitted, in any form, or by any means, electronic, mechanical, photocopying, recording or otherwise, without the prior permission of the publishers.

Copyright - Editions ENI - October 1999
ISBN: 2-7460-0535-2
Original edition: ISBN : 2-7460-0515-8

ENI Publishing LTD

500 Chiswick High Road
London W4 5RG

Tel. 020 8956 23 20
Fax. 020 8956 23 21
e-mail: publishing@ediENI.com
http://www.editions-eni.com

Editions ENI

BP 32125
44021 NANTES Cedex 1

Tél. 33.02.40.92.45.45
Fax. 33.02.40.92.45.46
e-mail : editions@ediENI.com
http://www.editions-eni.com

Author: Bruno GUERIN
Collection directed by Joëlle MUSSET
Translated from the French by Andrew BLACKBURN

Introduction — Chapter 1

A. Introduction **10**

B. Unix and Linux **11**

C. Principles of system administration **15**

Booting and halting the system — Chapter 2

A. Functioning principles of the init process **20**

B. Runlevels **21**

C. Initialization scripts **28**

D. Stopping and re-starting the system **32**

File systems — Chapter 3

A. What is a file system **41**

B. File systems on Linux **42**

C. The Linux file system: ext2fs **44**

D. Structure of an ext2fs file system **45**

kernel version 2.0 to 2.2

E.	The block: the unit of storage	**46**
F.	Structure of the superblock	**47**
G.	Structure of the block group descriptor	**50**
H.	Structure of an inode	**51**
I.	Structure of a datablock	**52**
J.	Creating a file system: **mke2fs**	**53**
K.	Mounting a file system: **mount**	**55**
L.	Unmounting a file system: **umount**	**61**
M.	Identifying processes that are using a file system: **fuser**	**62**
N.	Checking and repairing a file system: **fsck** . . .	**65**
O.	Swap management	**68**

User and group management — Chapter 4

- **A.** Creating a new account: an overview **73**
- **B.** Structure of the */etc/passwd* file **75**
- **C.** Structure of the */etc/shadow* file **77**
- **D.** Checking the */etc/passwd* and the */etc/shadow* files: **pwck** **78**
- **E.** Creating a user account: **useradd** **79**
- **F.** Group management **83**
- **G.** Modifying a user account: **usermod** **88**
- **H.** Deleting an account: **userdel** **89**
- **I.** Configuring user connections: **login** **90**
- **J.** Restricting terminal access **91**
- **K.** Limiting user resources **93**
- **L.** User information **95**

kernel version 2.0 to 2.2

Disk management — Chapter 5

A.	Special file names	**100**
B.	Listing the storage devices	**101**

Archiving and restoring — Chapter 6

A.	Archiving strategies	**105**
B.	Archiving and restoring utilities: **dump** and **restore**	**106**
C.	The **tar** command	**111**
D.	The **cpio** command	**113**
E.	**tar** versus **cpio**	**120**
F.	The **dd** command	**121**
G.	Tape management	**125**
H.	Remote archiving and restoring	**130**

Resource management — Chapter 7

- **A.** Monitoring system activity: **uptime, w** **135**
- **B.** Process management **137**
- **C.** Monitoring the memory and the CPU: **vmstat** **148**
- **D.** Disk space monitoring **151**
- **E.** Monitoring the swap: **swapon**, **free** **157**

Management of the printing system — Chapter 8

- **A.** The line printer daemon: **lpd** **161**
- **B.** Printer service configuration: */etc/printcap* **161**
- **C.** Control files **165**
- **D.** Printing command: **lpr** **168**
- **E.** Spool queue management: **lpq**, **lprm** **169**
- **F.** Administrating the printing system: **lpc** **170**
- **G.** Remote printing **173**

kernel version 2.0 to 2.2

Terminal management — Chapter 9

- **A.** Introduction **176**
- **B.** The **getty** daemon **177**
- **C.** Defining terminals **181**

Time and time zone management — Chapter 10

- **A.** Clock management: **clock**, **date** **190**
- **B.** Time zone management **193**

System accounting — Chapter 11

- **A.** Current sessions: **who** **200**
- **B.** History of user sessions: **last** **202**
- **C.** Reporting on user connection time: **ac** ... **205**
- **D.** Activating and de-activating process accounting: **accton** **206**
- **E.** Structure of the process accounting records ... **207**
- **F.** Using accounting information: **lastcomm**, **sa** ... **209**

Rebuilding the kernel — Chapter 12

- **A.** In which circumstances? **216**
- **B.** How? **217**
- **C.** Loadable modules **220**

  Index **229**

kernel version 2.0 to 2.2

Chapter 1

Introduction

A. Introduction 10

B. Unix and Linux 11

C. Principles of system administration 15

kernel version 2.0 to 2.2

A. Introduction

Linux is a Unix system which appeared in 1991. One of its main features is that it is totally free. However, Linux is not in the public domain, as it is covered by the FSF (Free Software Foundation) GNU "copyleft". This is a special license that was created to ensure that the source code remained freely accessible and would not be hindered by commercial interests. This copyleft allows complete freedom to anyone who wants to use, copy or modify the product under its protection, provided that the source code is always diffused freely and without hindrance.

Linux started as the hobby project of a student named Linus Torvalds who, using a lot of the GNU *(GNU is Not Unix)* software, finally produced what has become the most popular freely available operating system in the world.

Strictly speaking, Linux is not in itself, an operating system. It is a kernel, the *heart* of an operating system that forms the interface between the hardware and the set of commands, utilities and system programs that are necessary to make up the operating system. These latter components are provided either by the FSF or by third parties and are generally diffused and protected by the same copyleft.

You can install Linux in several ways:

– You can obtain from the Internet all the items you need to make up the system.
– Alternatively, you can use one of the numerous distributions that simplify the tasks of system installation and configuration.

For the beginner, the second solution is clearly preferable to the first. It must be noted, however, that distributions vary in the options they choose for basic commands and installable modules.

It is not our intention to suggest the use of one or another of these distributions as this is mainly a question of personal preference. The essential thing is to choose one of them and to get to know and master the Linux environment.

Once you are familiar with the Linux environment, it is easy to maintain the system, and to develop it safely without interrupting its operation. Consequently, the installation mode used has little importance when the system is customized (and therefore optimized), to suit the needs of the administrator and those of other users.

B. Unix and Linux

Linux is clearly not the same as Unix as it does not contain a single line of the code of the original Unix kernel of AT&T. However, Linux operates like a Unix system and the Linux kernel is by no means inferior to that of Unix. Above all, it must be remembered, that Linux is a kernel and the rest of the system comes from other sources. As a result, Linux may sometimes lack certain integrated graphical administration tools that are offered by most commercially available Unix systems. However, this is a minimal drawback as most of these tools are only interfaces between the administrator and the administration utilities, which work without them. Linux tools tend to be similar to each other and a good knowledge of them provides you with a better control of the system than you would obtain from graphical interfaces.

kernel version 2.0 to 2.2

In spite of the fact that its code has different origins, to all intents and purposes Linux *is* a fully-fledged Unix system. As far as day-to-day usage is concerned, there is no more difference between Linux and Unix than between two Unix systems. This remark is becoming increasingly pertinent as all Unix (and Linux) systems are converging as user commands conform increasingly to the POSIX standard.

What this book is not

This book is not an installation manual as installation instructions are specific to each distribution and are generally included in its accompanying documentation. However, the system is installed with a standard configuration which, while being perfectly functional and suitable for an individual user, may not meet fully more specific needs such as:

- definition of users and groups,
- login setting,
- installation and configuration of certain subsystems,
- archiving strategies,
- disk usage quotas,
- print management,
- terminal management,
- logging management,
- system accounting.

The general configuration has to provide a secure, coherent and productive system. However, to choose a suitable system configuration, you must first understand the various system components.

Chapter 1

What this book is

The principal objective of this book is to provide the Linux administrator with a thorough understanding of the various components and administrative tasks necessary to develop the Linux system.

We will not cover the graphical interface, which is based on X, the de facto Unix windowing system, nor will we describe the integrated administration tools. This is because we believe it is far more important and productive to have a sound knowledge of the standard utilities on which these tools are generally based. It is, therefore, on these utilities that the emphasis of this book will be placed.

Who this book is for

Basically, this book if for anyone who is in charge of a Linux system.

This book provides experienced Unix administrators with all the information they require on Linux specificities. It also provides beginners with all they need to know to administer the Linux system.

Unix in general and Linux in particular offers great power and flexibility. It must be noted, however, that the beginner will first need to spend a certain amount of time learning to handle this power.

Linux versions covered

Linux functions using two essential elements: the kernel and the system libraries, of which the most important is **libc**.

kernel version 2.0 to 2.2

This is a time of great progress in the Linux world. For example, the following two elements have been undergoing a quantum leap:

- When Linux version 2.2.0 was released, it was shortly followed by a set of patches to reach version to 2.2.5: This kernel provides a large number of improvements and innovations for example, improved support for drivers and multi-processor systems.
- The **libc** library has been undergoing a veritable revolution. For a long time, Linux was accompanied by a specific library (of which the last version was **libc** 5.4.4.46). Recently however, the GNU team implemented a major project called **glibc-2**, with the objective of providing a universal standard library for systems such as Linux, Hurd and FreeBSD... The most common versions are the **glibc-2.x** range. **glibc-2.1** appeared in February 1999, offering not only its own set of innovations and improvements, but also a more advanced integration of standards such as POSIX and Unix98. In this way it made an important contribution to the harmonization of the different Unix systems.

C. Principles of system administration

The system administrator is responsible for the following tasks:

- system booting and shutdown
- management of existing users
- adding users
- removing users
- modifying user characteristics
- archive planning and management
- peripherals management
- adding and removing printers
- adding and removing disk devices
- terminal configuration
- software management
- kernel maintenance
- updating of kernel source
- integrating new peripheral devices
- management of resident modules
- system security.

In all cases, the administrator is responsible for maintaining the system to ensure that users can work productively and in complete confidence.

kernel version 2.0 to 2.2

↓personal notes↓

Chapter 2

Booting and halting the system

A. Functioning principles of the init process ... 20

B. Runlevels 21
  1. Single user mode 21
  2. Multi-user mode 22
  3. The runlevel concept 22
  4. The /etc/inittab file 23

C. Initialization scripts 28
  1. Redhat Initialization scripts 28
  2. Slackware Initialization scripts 31

D. Stopping and re-starting the system 32
  1. The **shutdown** command 32
  2. The **halt** and **reboot** commands 35
  3. The **poweroff** command 37
  4. Rebooting from single user mode 37

kernel version 2.0 to 2.2

When speaking of starting the system, the terms boot (short for bootstrap), bootup and startup are used indifferently.

The boot process puts the system in a known stable and usable state. It generally involves three main phases:
— POST (Power-On Self Test) hardware diagnostics,
— Loading the kernel into memory,
— Starting various system programs as appropriate (for example Web Servers).

On a PC, hardware analysis is generally carried out by the BIOS (Basic Input/Output System). This is a small program, generally placed in a flash ROM that can be updated.

The POST step generally ends by loading the program from block 0 of the first hard disk. This block is called MBR (Master Boot Record).

The Linux kernel is called **vmlinuz** and is usually stored either in /boot or directly in the top level (root) directory. To economize diskspace, **vmlinuz** is stored in compressed format and is decompressed on loading (this is the reason for the final **z** of the name, which is a suffix used for certain compressed files).

*The name **vmlinuz** originates from BSD systems, on which the kernel is stored in compressed format in the /vmunix or the /vmuniz file.*

Kernel sizes can vary according to the configuration options that were chosen when it was compiled. When it was compiled as we shall see later, it is possible to produce a standard kernel containing the bare minimum to allow the system to boot. Drivers are then loaded as and when they are required.

Chapter 2

The kernel carries out a set of diagnostic tests and initializations on peripheral devices. During this phase, a number of messages scroll up on the screen. So that you can read them, these messages are stored temporarily in the */proc/kmsg* file. They can be viewed using the **dmesg** utility.

When the initializations have been carried out, the kernel starts **init**. This is the first system process. It is the parent of all the other processes on Unix in general and on Linux in particular. Moreover, **init** is the direct parent of login shells on serial and virtual terminals.

This process functions similarly to its System V counterpart. Its basic difference with respect to that of the BSD branch is that the Linux **init** uses a file that allows you to define the general functioning of the system, including its runlevels.

A. Functioning principles of the init process

The **init** process is the last phase of system startup. It implements certain initializations and starts a number of daemon processes that provide subsystems and services.

The main initializations and configurations include:
- checking file system integrity using the */etc/fstab* file that contains a static description of the file systems,
- mounting of these file systems,
- activation of paging partitions,
- configuration of the network interface card (or cards in the case of a router).

init starts a certain number of processes including:
- the logging utilities **syslogd** (system logging) and **klogd** (kernel logging),
- the line printer daemon **lpd** (spool area handler),
- the Internet superserver (**inetd**),
- the various **rpc** daemons for the NFS (Network File System),
- a number of **getty** daemons to manage serial and virtual terminals,
- the **sendmail** electronic mail transport agent,
- the **cron** daemon to run commands defined in the crontab files in the */var/spool/cron* directory. These files are named after user accounts.
- site specific daemons set up by the system administrator, such as web servers, samba server, firewall managers...

The Unix BSD version of **init** carries out its required actions by executing the following two scripts successively: */etc/rc* and */etc/rc.local*.

The System V version, which is used with RedHat distributions, also works with scripts. However, in this case **init** consults the /etc/inittab file to decide which scripts to execute. This file also allows extended use of runlevel techniques.

B. Runlevels

Originally, Unix had three runlevels:
- "out of service" level
- single user (or maintenance mode)
- multi user (or normal mode).

1. Single user mode

In this functional state only one user can login at a time.

This mode may be chosen for a number of reasons. Here are the most common ones:
- to resolve hardware or software technical problems,
- to install or configure a new peripheral,
- to build a new kernel with enhanced functionalities.

While carrying out any of these tasks you must ensure that no one else uses the system. Also in some cases, it may be essential to work with a minimal system configuration (with only the main file system installed, without any of the subsystems running).

kernel version 2.0 to 2.2

To start Linux in maintenance mode, enter **linux single** in response to the **boot** prompt:

```
boot : linux single
```

As we shall see later, you can also go into single user mode when you are already in normal (multi-user) mode.

2. Multi-user mode

This is the normal system functioning mode. It allows several users to access the system and installed resources such as the print subsystem and the network.

3. The runlevel concept

The **init** version most commonly used on Linux is that from the Miquel van Smoorenburg, **sysvinit** software suite. It is based on the System V concept of runlevels. This is an extension of the two principal functioning modes outlined above. A runlevel is a system configuration that allows only a specific group of processes to run. There are eight basic runlevels identified by the numbers 0 to 6 and the letter s (or S). Runlevels **0,1** and **6** are reserved as follows: runlevel 0 is used to halt the system, runlevel **6** is used to reboot it, runlevel **1** is used to put the system into single user mode. Runlevel **s** is used to execute scripts while in single user mode. The definitions of runlevels **2**, **3**, **4** and **5** depend on the specific system or distribution.

The **init** process consults the /etc/inittab file to find out which actions it must carry out for the runlevel specified.

4. The /etc/inittab file

This file is made up of a number of entries, one per line. Each entry defines a process together with its execution parameters. Empty lines are ignored, as are those beginning with a hash (#) character (this character allows you to add useful comments).

An entry is made up of four fields, separated by colons (:):

Id is the field identifier, a sequence of 1 to 4 characters. It is usually two characters long and must be unique in the file.

Runlevels lists the runlevels concerned by the entry. If this field is empty, the action (see **action**) will be carried out for all runlevels. The runlevel list is made up of runlevel identifiers, written one after the other. In the following example the action specified must be taken for runlevels 1, 2, 3 and 5:

```
c1:1235:respawn:/sbin/getty tty1 VC linux
```

action specifies how process execution must be carried out. You can specify one of the following functions:

- **respawn** The process will be re-started each time it terminates.
- **wait** When **init** goes into the runlevel concerned, the specified process (see **Process**) is started and **init** waits for it to terminate before continuing.
- **once** The specified process will be started only once. Consequently, it will not be started if it is already running.
- **boot** The process will be started during system boot. Consequently, runlevels (defined in the second field) will be ignored.

bootwait	The same as **boot** except that **init** will wait for the process to terminate.
off	Nothing is run. This specification allows you to create entries without activating them.
ondemand	The same as **respawn** except that it is associated with the specified **ondemand** runlevels (which can be a, b and/or c). This allows you to request **init** to execute the associated process without any change of runlevel occurring (by specifying the **ondemand** runlevels).
initdefault	Specifies the runlevel by default after system boot. If /etc/inittab contains no entry which has **initdefault** specified in the **action** field, the default runlevel must be indicated by the administrator from the console keyboard. If this function is specified, the **process** field is ignored as this entry does not execute a process.
sysinit	The process concerned will be executed during system boot, before any entries marked as **boot** and **bootwait**. As with these entries, the **runlevels** field is ignored.
powerwait	The process concerned is executed when **init** receives the SIGPWR signal. **init** waits for it to terminate before continuing.

	powerfail	The same as **powerwait** except that **init** does not wait for the process concerned to terminate before continuing.
	powerokwait	The process concerned is executed when **init** receives the SIGPWR signal, provided that the */etc/powerstatus* file exists and contains the word **OK** (this indicates that the power is back on).
	ctrlaltdel	The process concerned is executed when **init** receives the SIGINT signal. This signal is sent when the [Ctrl][Alt][Del] key combination is pressed on the system console. Generally, a shutdown process will be specified in the **process** field of this entry, either to go into single user mode, or to reboot the system.
Process		specifies the process to be executed, including its path.

In addition, a comment can be added at the end of the entry following a hash (#) character. Here is an extract from the */etc/inittab* file:

```
# Default runlevel.
id:4:initdefault:

# System initialization (runs when system boots).
si:S:sysinit:/etc/rc.d/rc.S

# Script to run when going single user (runlevel 1).
su:1S:wait:/etc/rc.d/rc.K

# Script to run when going multi user.
rc:23456:wait:/etc/rc.d/rc.M

# What to do at the "Three Finger Salute".
ca::ctrlaltdel:/sbin/shutdown -t5 -rfn now
# Runlevel 0 halts the system.l0:0:wait:/etc/rc.d/rc.0
# Runlevel 6 reboots the system.
l6:6:wait:/etc/rc.d/rc.6


# What to do when power fails
pf::powerfail:/sbin/shutdown -fh +2 "THE POWER IS FAILING"

# If power is back before shutdown, cancel the running
shutdown.
pg:0123456:powerokwait:/root/scripts/shutdown -c
"THE POWER IS BACK"

# If power comes back in single user mode, return to
multi user mode.
ps:S:powerokwait:/sbin/init 5

c1:1235:respawn:/sbin/getty tty1 VC linux
c2:1235:respawn:/sbin/getty tty2 VC linux
c3:12345:respawn:/sbin/getty tty3 VC linux
c4:12345:respawn:/sbin/getty tty4 VC linux
c5:12345:respawn:/sbin/getty tty5 VC linux
c6:12345:respawn:/sbin/getty tty6 VC linux
c7:12345:respawn:/sbin/getty tty7 VC linux
c8:12345:respawn:/sbin/getty tty8 VC linux

x1:4:wait:/etc/rc.d/rc.4
```

*The /etc/inittab file is read by **init**, when init is started. **init** must be asked to re-read the /etc/inittab file so that it will apply any changes that have been made to it by the system administrator. You can ask **init** to re-read this file by sending it the SIGHUP signal as follows:*
```
# kill -HUP 1
```

Finding out the current runlevel

The **runlevel** command displays both the current and previous system runlevels:

```
[9]-system(merlin)~:runlevel
N 4
```

The `N` in the above example indicates that there was no previous runlevel (the system has used only one runlevel since booting).

Changing the runlevel

Use the following syntax to change the runlevel:
```
init NEW_RUNLEVEL
```

for example:
```
# init 5
# runlevel
4 5
```

C. Initialization scripts

Generally, each level has an initialization script associated with it. These scripts depend on the distribution used for system installation. There are two basic initialization script organizations:

- that of the **Redhat** distribution, which conforms fairly well to the System V standard.
- that of the **Slackware** distribution, which is more simplified and similar to that of BSD and AIX.

1. Redhat Initialization scripts

These scripts are grouped together in the /etc/rc.d directory:

```
[4]-system(morgan)/etc/rc.d:ls -l
total 18
drwxr-xr-x   2 root     root         1024 Nov 20 22:48 init.d
-rwxr-xr-x   1 root     root         1593 Jul  1  1998 rc
-rwxr-xr-x   1 root     root          690 Jul  1  1998 rc.local
-rwxr-xr-x   1 root     root         6514 Jul  1  1998 rc.sysinit
drwxr-xr-x   2 root     root         1024 Feb  5 22:38 rc0.d
drwxr-xr-x   2 root     root         1024 Nov 20 22:48 rc1.d
drwxr-xr-x   2 root     root         1024 Nov 20 22:48 rc2.d
drwxr-xr-x   2 root     root         1024 Nov 20 22:55 rc3.d
drwxr-xr-x   2 root     root         1024 Nov 20 22:55 rc4.d
drwxr-xr-x   2 root     root         1024 Nov 20 22:55 rc5.d
drwxr-xr-x   2 root     root         1024 Nov 20 22:48 rc6.d
```

This directory contains the three scripts **rc, rc.local** and **rc.sysinit**, along with a number of subdirectories.

The **rc.sysinit** script is the first to be run, as shown by the /etc/inittab file extract below:

```
id:3:initdefault:

# System initialization.
si::sysinit:/etc/rc.d/rc.sysinit

l0:0:wait:/etc/rc.d/rc 0
l1:1:wait:/etc/rc.d/rc 1
l2:2:wait:/etc/rc.d/rc 2
l3:3:wait:/etc/rc.d/rc 3
l4:4:wait:/etc/rc.d/rc 4
l5:5:wait:/etc/rc.d/rc 5
l6:6:wait:/etc/rc.d/rc 6
```

The **rc** script determines the actions to be carried out each time the system changes runlevel. **rc** runs the scripts contained in the rcN.d directories, where N corresponds to the runlevel it receives as an argument.

The **rc.local** script usually contains configuration commands that are specific to the site on which the system is installed.

In each of these rcN.d subdirectories, there are two types of script:

```
[12]-system(morgan)/etc/rc.d:ls -X rc3.d/
K15gpm      K80random    S10network   S40portmap   S60nfs
K20rusersd  K95nfsfs     S30syslog    S40snmpd     S75keytable
K20rwhod    K96pcmcia    S40atd       S50inet      S80sendmail
K55routed   S01kerneld   S40crond     S60lpd       S99local
```

— Scripts starting with an S (Start) are those that are run when the system goes into the runlevel (N) concerned.
— Scripts starting with a K (Kill) are those that are run when the system leaves the runlevel (N) concerned.

The number and the name following the initial letter, allow the system to determine the execution order for each script. For example, the `S40atd` script is started after the `S30syslog` script and before the `S40crond` script.

A number of scripts are common to several runlevels. To avoid any duplication, all the scripts are stored only in the /etc/rc.d/init.d directory, while the rcN.d subdirectories contain symbolic links to these scripts. This technique simplifies the maintenance of these scripts:

```
[18]-system(morgan)/etc/rc.d:ls -X init.d/
atd           kerneld      nfsfs        rwhod
crond         keytable     pcmcia       sendmail
functions     killall      portmap      single
gpm           lpd          random       snmpd
halt          network      routed       syslog
inet          nfs          rusersd      initservices.desc
[19]-system(morgan)/etc/rc.d:ls -l rc3.d/|tr -s " "
|cut -d" " -f9-
K15gpm -> ../init.d/gpm
K20rusersd -> ../init.d/rusersd
K20rwhod -> ../init.d/rwhod
K55routed -> ../init.d/routed
K80random -> ../init.d/random
K95nfsfs -> ../init.d/nfsfs
K96pcmcia -> ../init.d/pcmcia
S01kerneld -> ../init.d/kerneld
S10network -> ../init.d/network
S30syslog -> ../init.d/syslog
S40atd -> ../init.d/atd
S40crond -> ../init.d/crond
S40portmap -> ../init.d/portmap
S40snmpd -> ../init.d/snmpd
S50inet -> ../init.d/inet
S60lpd -> ../init.d/lpd
S60nfs -> ../init.d/nfs
S75keytable -> ../init.d/keytable
S80sendmail -> ../init.d/sendmail
S99local -> ../rc.local
```

Although this architecture may appear complex, it is in fact very convenient to use. You can easily identify the script you want to modify in /etc/rc.d/init.d. Then, thanks to the symbolic links, any changes you make will be applied immediately on each runlevel concerned.

2. Slackware Initialization scripts

In contrast to the approach described above, the Slackware distribution stores a restricted number of scripts in a single directory (/etc/rc.d):

```
[25]-system(merlin)/etc/rc.d:ls -l
total 41
lrwxrwxrwx   1 root     root           4 Sep 17  1997 rc.0 - rc.6
-rwxr-xr-x   1 root     root         396 Oct  2  1995 rc.4*
-rwxr-xr-x   1 root     root        2435 Mar 10 23:41 rc.6*
-rwxr-xr-x   1 root     root        1234 Jan 19 22:11 rc.K*
-rwxr-xr-x   1 root     root        3139 Dec 13  1997 rc.M*
-rwxr-xr-x   1 root     root        4365 Mar 29 22:17 rc.S*
-rwxr-xr-x   1 root     root        1175 Jul  7  1996 rc.cdrom*
-rwxr-xr-x   1 root     root         122 Sep 17  1997 rc.font*
-rwxr-xr-x   1 root     root          64 Apr 28  1996 rc.ibcs2*
-rwxr-xr-x   1 root     root        1982 Jul 28  1998 rc.inet1*
-rwxr-xr-x   1 root     root        2907 Mar 20 16:09 rc.inet2*
-rwxr-xr--   1 root     root          17 Sep 23  1997 rc.keymap*
-rwxr-xr-x   1 root     root        1589 Mar 10 23:44 rc.local*
-rwxr-xr-x   1 root     root        5324 Apr 19 17:35 rc.modules*
-rwxr-xr-x   1 root     root        8121 Apr 30  1995 rc.serial*
```

Here is the corresponding *inittab* file:

```
# Default runlevel.
id:4:initdefault:

# System initialization (runs when system boots).
si:S:sysinit:/etc/rc.d/rc.S

# Script to run when going single user (runlevel 1).
su:1S:wait:/etc/rc.d/rc.K

# Script to run when going multi user.
rc:23456:wait:/etc/rc.d/rc.M

# Runlevel 0 halts the system.
l0:0:wait:/etc/rc.d/rc.0

# Runlevel 6 reboots the system.
l6:6:wait:/etc/rc.d/rc.6
```

D. Stopping and re-starting the system

The system must never be stopped by cutting the power off. Certain data is stored in memory rather than on disk and the system must ensure coherence between the two. It does this by using the **update** daemon notably, which forces this coherence every 30 seconds by default.

Consequently, if the system is stopped abruptly, the daemons concerned will not have time to update the disk correctly. In addition, any data that has been modified recently by logged-in users will also be lost.

To avoid these problems, the system must be stopped using the commands provided for this purpose:
- shutdown
- halt
- reboot
- poweroff.

1. The **shutdown** command

This is a BSD-type command that is used on SunOS, Digital UNIX and AIX systems. In common with the other starting and stopping utilities, **shutdown** is a member of the **sysvinit** software suite.

shutdown allows you to stop the system, to re-start it or to go into maintenance mode. Here is the syntax of this command:
```
shutdown [options] time [message]
```

The `time` argument can be specified in several formats:
- The `hh:mm` format indicates the time at which the **shutdown** must take place.
- The `[+]m` format indicates the number of minutes that must elapse before the shutdown procedure is started.
- The word `now` starts the shutdown procedure immediately (`now` is an alias for +0). This format must be used only when you are sure that there are no other sessions running.

You can specify the text of the message that will be sent to all users. Otherwise a default message will be sent according to the type of shutdown specified.

Here is an example of the default message sent when you ask the system to re-start:

```
Broadcast message from root (ttyp1) Thu Mar 18 21:20:57 1999...
The system is going DOWN for reboot in 51 minutes !!
```

Here is an example of the default message sent when you ask the system to halt:

```
Broadcast message from root (ttyp1) Thu Mar 18 21:20:57 1999...
The system is going DOWN for halt in 5 minutes !!
```

Calling the **shutdown** command without an option puts the system in maintenance mode. This command calls the **init 1** command, which warns the users and leaves them time to save their data and close their sessions properly.

The following options can be used with the **shutdown** command:

- `-c` cancels the current **shutdown** command that is currently running. If you specify this option you cannot indicate a `time` argument. However you can supply a message to explain to the users why the shutdown has been cancelled. No message is sent by default.
- `-f` specifies a rapid system re-start (see the remark below concerning this option).
- `-h` halts the system after shutdown.
- `-k` does not shutdown the system. All this option does it to send the warning messages to the users.
- `-r` reboots the system after shutdown.
- `-t N` specifies a wait of `N` seconds between sending the SIGTERM signal and sending the SIGKILL signal to active processes. By default, this delay is 30 seconds.

If a shutdown procedure is started with a delay (other than `now`), a /etc/nologin file is created containing the message generated by the **shutdown** command. This file is created either immediately or five minutes before shutdown. The presence of this file prevents all users other than root from logging-in. Any user login attempts will be refused and the contents of the /etc/nologin file will be displayed on the user's terminal.

The login program of the shadow suite will check the presence of the /etc/nologin file only if it is requested to do so in its /etc/login.defs configuration file.

The /etc/nologin file is automatically deleted if the shutdown procedure is cancelled.

When the -f option is specified, **shutdown** creates the /fastboot file. The presence of this file is detected on the next boot and the **fsck** file system checking utility is not run (cf. Chapter 3, section N, Checking and repairing file systems).

The -c option provides a very convenient means of canceling a shutdown procedure. On many systems, the only way to do this is to search for the PID of the shutdown process and send it a termination signal using the **kill** command. Here is an example of this command used on a BSD system:

```
# kill `ps aux | grep shutdown`
```

The **shutdown** command of the sysvinit suite writes its PID in the /var/run/shutdown.pid file when a halt or a reboot is requested. This technique allows the system to stop a shutdown process very conveniently. It also allows the system to ensure that only one shutdown process is running at once.

2. The **halt** and **reboot** commands

The **halt** command stops the system rapidly, while the **reboot** command stops and restarts the system rapidly. In fact, **reboot** is a symbolic link to **halt** that requests system re-start.

Normally, these comands should be executed when the system is in either runlevel 0 or 6. They are used in the last script executed when the process is in runlevel 0 or 6, and the system must be stopped or re-started (this script is (*/etc/rc.d/rc.[06]* for a Slackware distribution, or */etc/rc.d/init.d/halt* for a Redhat distribution). They should not be called directly in normal mode (when the runlevel is neither 0 nor 6). However, if they are started in normal mode they will call either **shutdown h** or **shutdown r**. Normally, all **halt** and **reboot** do is to update the */var/adm/wtmp* file, synchronize the disks with the buffers, and either halt or reboot the system.

These commands offer the following options:

- `-d` The */var/adm/wtmp* file is not updated.
- `-f` The halt or reboot is forced without calling **shutdown**.
- `-n` The disks are not synchronized before halting or rebooting (this option also implies `-d`).
- `-p` If a halt was requested, a poweroff is executed (where possible).
- `-w` Only the */var/adm/wtmp* file is updated and no halt or reboot takes place.

It is very dangerous to use the `-f` option. This is practically the same as cutting the power off. It means that the file systems will not be unmounted properly, and that the processes will not be correctly terminated...

The `-n` option is useful after system restructuring by **fsck**. This is because **fsck** works directly on the disk, and a normal stoppage would overwrite the superblock by the (erroneous) memory copy.

The `-p` option is not available with **reboot** because it would prevent the system from re-starting itself.

3. The **poweroff** command

This command is also a link to **halt**, this time with the -p option. It stops the system rapidly and powers down (provided that the motherboard is equipped with a software power off mechanism). **poweroff** provides the same options as **halt**.

4. Rebooting from single user mode

There are two basic ways of rebooting from maintenance mode. You can use either the [Ctrl] D key combination, or the **shutdown** or **reboot** command.

The [Ctrl] D key combination starts the boot procedure immediately and no disk checking is carried out. On the other hand, **shutdown** or **reboot** stops the system before rebooting it in multi-user mode. In this case, the system is reinitialized and a full reboot is carried out.

kernel version 2.0 to 2.2

↓personal notes↓

Chapter 3

File systems

A.	What is a file system	**41**
B.	File systems on Linux	**42**
C.	The Linux file system: ext2fs	**44**
D.	Structure of an ext2fs file system	**45**
E.	The block: the unit of storage	**46**
F.	Structure of the superblock	**47**
G.	Structure of the block group descriptor	**50**
H.	Structure of an inode	**51**
I.	Structure of a datablock	**52**
J.	Creating a file system: **mke2fs**	**53**
K.	Mounting a file system: **mount**	**55**
	1. Listing the mounted file systems: /etc/mtab . . .	**56**
	2. Mounting a file system manually	**56**
	3. The /etc/fstab file	**58**
	4. Mounting file systems automatically	**61**

kernel version 2.0 to 2.2

L. Unmounting a file system: **umount** **61**

M. Identifying processes that are using
    a file system: **fuser** **62**

N. Checking and repairing a file system: **fsck** .   **65**
    1. **fsck** functionality **66**
    2. **fsck** options **67**

O. Swap management **68**
    1. Setting up a swap area: **mkswap** **68**
    2. Activating a swap area: **swapon** **69**
    3. Deactivating a swap area: **swapoff** **70**

A. What is a file system

A file system is a means of organizing and storing directories and files on disk. Each disk partition, or non-partitioned disk, has its own file system.

> *It is possible to aggregate several file systems so that they will be seen as one (band and partition aggregation).*

Each file/directory has a unique reference made up of two numbers:

- a peripheral **device identifier**. This references the peripheral device, and therefore the file system, in which the file/directory is stored.
- a file descriptor or **inode**. This provides a unique reference of the file/directory within the file system.

All file systems maintain inode tables. These tables reference all the files contained in the file system and allow the operating system to manage them. An inode is a structure that contains information on access permissions and data-blocks occupied by the file. The unique **file identifier** is the index of the file in the inode table.

Thanks to this architecture, the file system is independent of the disk or partition organization.

The file system structure is vitally important to the **data transfer rate** of input/output operations and to the file systems' recovery possibilities after a crash of the operating system.

The data transfer rate, or throughput, announced by the peripheral device manufacturer is a vital piece of information. However, it is not sufficient to indicate operational input/output performance as this also depends on how the data is structured on the disk.

kernel version 2.0 to 2.2

Moreover, the complete file set may be spread over several file systems. This may be done for several reasons relating to disk space constraints or organizational preferences of the system administrator:

- the system has been configured on several disks to provide fault tolerance and performance. However, the RAID (Redundant Array of Independent Disks) concept allows Linux to consider several disks as a single file system.
- the disk space occupied is too large for one file system,
- to limit loss of data risks in the case of file system deterioration,
- to enhance access performance,
- to limit the disk space occupied.

B. File systems on Linux

Linux can manage a large number of file systems:

- Apple Macintosh file system,
- MS-DOS file system,
- Windows 95, Windows 98 and Windows NT 4, non compressed FAT (File Allocation Table) systems,
- Windows NT NTFS (NT File System) (in read-only mode from version 2.2),
- ISO9660 file systems (for CD ROM),
- Minix file system,
- OS/2, HPFS file system,
- File systems for Unix System V and SCO,
- UFS file system for Unix BSD, SunOS, FreeBSD and NextStep,
- Amiga FFS File system.

The distinction must be clearly drawn between the file systems that Linux is capable of working with, and those that the Linux kernel installed is actually able to manage. The latter, which are generally a subset of the former. They are listed in the /proc/filesystems file:

```
[396]-system(merlin)~:cat /proc/filesystems
         ext2
         minix
         msdos
         vfat
nodev    proc
nodev    nfs
nodev    smbfs
         iso9660
         xenix
         sysv
         coherent
         ntfs
         hfs
nodev    autofs
```

The Linux standard file system is called **ext2fs**. This file system will be introduced in the next section.

C. The Linux file system: ext2fs

The Linux file system is called **ext2fs** (second extended file system). **ext2fs** is an extension of **ext** which itself is an extension of **Minix**, the original Linux file system. A comparison of these three file systems is outlined in the table below:

Characteristics	Minix	Ext	Ext2fs
Maximum size of the file system	64 Mbytes	2 Gbytes	4 Tbytes
Maximum size of a file	64 Mbytes	2 Gbtytes	2 Gbytes
Maximum size of a file name	14 char.	255 char.	255 char.
Support of the three Unix timestamps	No	No	Yes
Extension possibilities	No	No	Yes
Variable block-size	No	No	Yes

In common with all Unix file systems, **ext2fs** supports the standard functions (regular files, directories, special files, symbolic links...). In addition, it offers the following advanced functions:

- Supplementary attributes that allow you to modify the functioning of the kernel according to the files concerned.
- Compatibility with System V or BSD concerning the owner group of newly created files and directories. System V compatibility is provided by default (all files and directories are created as members of the same group as the process that created them). Alternatively, a mounting option allows you to choose a BSD type functioning, whereby the group is inherited from the parent directory and not from the creating process.
- Rapid symbolic links. The name of the file that is pointed to by the symbolic link is written directly in the inode of the link and not in a data-block. This technique accelerates the resolution of the link.

- You can pass a parameter to the kernel so that, in case of error, it will:
  - do nothing and continue normally,
  - re-mount the file system in read only mode so as not to risk corrupting the data,
  - provoke a "kernel panic" type error.
- A number of other options can be specified when creating an **ext2fs** file system. These will be covered in the "Creating a file system: mke2fs" section.

D. Structure of an ext2fs file system

Here is the general physical layout of the **ext2fs** file system:

Boot sector	Block Group 1	Block Group 2	....	Block Group N

An **ext2fs** file system is made up of boot sector and several groups of blocks. The boot sector has a structure similar to that of the block groups. It contains the instruction sequence that is required to load the kernel when the system is booted.

Each block group has the following structure:

Super block	Group descriptors	Block bitmap	Inode bitmap	Inode table	Data blocks

kernel version 2.0 to 2.2

- The **superblock** is a structure that contains control information on the file system (basic size and shape). The **superblock** is present in the boot sector. It is also duplicated in each block group for easy recovery in case of file system corruption.
- The **group descriptor** is a data structure that describes the block group. It also stores the addresses of blocks containing vital information such as bitmaps and the **inode table**. Each block group contains the group descriptors of all block groups. Again, this is done for security reasons.
- The **blocks bitmap** is a table of bits. Each bit in this table corresponds to a block and indicates whether it is free or occupied. This table is used for block allocation and de-allocation.
- The **inodes bitmap** is also a table of bits. Each bit in this table corresponds to an inode and indicates whether it is free or occupied. This table is used for inode allocation and de-allocation.

E. The block: the unit of storage

The block is an important concept concerning peripheral storage devices. A clear distinction must be made between a physical block (512 bytes, for example) and a logical block (1, 2, 4 or 8 Kbytes).

A physical block is the physical unit of storage. For Linux, the size of a physical block is 1 Kbyte. Other Unix systems allow you to choose different sizes when you create the file system.

File sizes are always expressed in multiples of the block size. Any unused space in an occupied block cannot be used by another file. Consequently, small block sizes optimize disk space usage. This is especially true when the file system contains large numbers of small files. However, small block sizes also penalize transfer performance for large files.

F. Structure of the superblock

The superblock structure is defined in the /usr/include/linux/ext2_fs.h file. It includes the following elements:

Description	Size (bytes)
Total number of inodes	4
Total number of blocks	4
Number of blocks reserved for root	4
Number of free blocks	4
Number of free inodes	4
Number of the first data block	4
(Logical) block size	4
Fragment size	4
Number of blocks per group	4
Number of fragments per group	4
Number of inodes per group	4
Last file system mount time	4
Last superblock write time	4
Number of times the file system has been mounted since last check	2
Maximum number file system mountings before forced check	2

kernel version 2.0 to 2.2

Description	Size (bytes)
Magic signature (number), identifying the file system	2
State of the file system (clean/not clean mount)	2
Functioning procedure in case of errors	2
Minor revision level	2
Time of last check	4
Maximum interval between checks	4
Creator of operating system	4
Revision level	2
Default UID for blocks reserved for root	2
Default GID for blocks reserved for root	2

In common with most Unix systems, Linux always works with a copy of the superblock in memory. This is done for performance reasons. Linux updates the disk periodically at what are called synchronization points. Consequently, an abrupt halt of the system can result in the file system becoming corrupted. In certain circumstances, the synchronization must be forced (notably when the system is stopped using the **shutdown** *command for example). In addition, you can synchronize at any time using the* **sync** *command.*

You can view the contents of the superblock by calling the **tune2fs** command with the `-l` option, as in the following example:

```
[merlin]# tune2fs -l /dev/hdc2
tune2fs 1.12, 9-Jul-98 for EXT2 FS 0.5b, 95/08/09
Filesystem volume name:   <none>
Last mounted on:          <not available>
Filesystem UUID:          6f729cca-8aee-11d2-9608-c86ffb8e4f4a
Filesystem magic number:  0xEF53
Filesystem revision #:    0 (original)
Filesystem features:      (none)
Filesystem state:         not clean
Errors behavior:          Continue
Filesystem OS type:       Linux
Inode count:              359800
Block count:              1433601
Reserved block count:     71694
Free blocks:              200169
Free inodes:              301000
First block:              1
Block size:               1024
Fragment size:            1024
Blocks per group:         8192
Fragments per group:      8192
Inodes per group:         2056
Inode blocks per group:   257
Last mount time:          Fri Apr 30 22:34:37 1999
Last write time:          Mon May  3 10:04:55 1999
Mount count:              9
Maximum mount count:      20
Last checked:             Mon Apr 19 13:46:44 1999
Check interval:           0 (<none>)
Reserved blocks uid:      0 (user root)
Reserved blocks gid:      0 (group root)
```

G. Structure of the block group descriptor

This structure is defined in the */usr/include/linux/ext2_fs.h* file. It includes the following elements:

Description	Size (bytes)
Address of the blocks bitmap for the blocks of this group	4
Address of the inodes bitmap for the inodes of this group	4
Address of the first block of the inodes table for this block group	4
Number of free blocks for this group	2
Number of free inodes for this group	2
Not used	2
Reserved for future extensions	12

H. Structure of an inode

Each file is associated with an inode. However, several files can be attached to the same inode. This allows you to create links to a file using the **ln** command.

The first inode in the inode table is always unused and the second corresponds to the root directory. The size of an inode is 64 bytes. It includes the following elements:

File type and permissions (2 bytes)
Number of links (2 bytes)
UID (2 bytes)
GID (2 bytes)
File size in bytes (2 bytes)
Last access timestamp (4 bytes)
Last modification timestamp (4 bytes)
Last inode modification timestamp (4 bytes)
Table of 15 datablock pointers (3 bytes) containing:
12 direct data pointers
1 indirect data pointer
1 double indirect data pointer
1 triple indirect data pointer

Concerning the data-block pointers:

- the 12 direct data pointers contain the data-block numbers (addresses),
- the indirect data pointer contains the address of a block containing 128 addresses of data-blocks,
- the double indirect data pointer contains the address of a block containing 128 addresses of indirect data-blocks,
- the triple data pointer contains the address of a block containing 128 addresses of double indirect data-blocks.

kernel version 2.0 to 2.2

Consequently, the maximum size of a Unix file is:

Size = (12 * LB) + (128 * LB) + (128 * 128 * LB) + (128 * 128 * 128 * LB)

where:

LB is the size of a logical block.

For example, if LB = 512 bytes, the maximum file size is approximately 1 Gbyte.

I. Structure of a datablock

There are three types of block according to what the block contains:

— block of data
— block of pointers
— free block.

Blocks of data are associated with ordinary files and are made up of an unstructured string of bytes.

For directories, these are information blocks concerning the files contained in the directory. When a directory is created, it contains two entries, called "." and "..":

. for which the inode is that of the created directory,

.. for which the inode is that of the parent directory.

A directory file is a list of directory entries. Each directory entry contains the following elements:

Inode for this directory entry (4 Bytes)
Size of this entry (2 Bytes)
Name length for this directory entry (2 Bytes)
File name (*n* Bytes)

J. Creating a file system: **mke2fs**

In general, before you can use a peripheral storage device such as a hard disk, you must create a file system on it (a possible exception to this rule is when you use the **dump**, **tar** or **cpio** archiving utilities).

Every file system has a creation command associated with it. However, Linux cannot create directly, all the file systems it can manage. Here are some of the file systems that Linux can create:

- **ext2fs**, using the **mke2fs** or **mkfs.ext2** command
- **minix**, using the **mkfs.minix** command,
- **msdos**, using the **mkdosfs** or **mkfs.msdos** command
- **xfs**, using the **mkxfs** or **mkfs.xiafs** command (Linux no longer supports the **ext** and **xiafs** file systems, as from version 2.1.21 of the Linux kernel).

In this chapter we will describe the creation of a **ext2fs** file system using **mke2fs**.

Here is the syntax of the **mke2fs** command:

```
mke2fs [OPTIONS] SPECIAL_FILE
```

The following options are available:

- `-b N1` To specify the block size (`N1`) in bytes.
- `-c` To check the peripheral for bad blocks before creating the file system. We strongly advise the use of this option.
- `-f N2` To specify the fragment size (`N2`) in bytes. This option is accepted even when the block fragmentation has not yet been implemented.
- `-i N3` To specify how many bytes per inode (`N3`). This value is a minimum of 1024, and it defaults to 4096. This value allows you to adjust the maximum number of files that the file system can contain according to the average file size. The smaller this average size, the smaller the bytes per inode ratio should be.
- `-l FILE` To specify the name of the file containing the bad blocks list. This list must have been created previously (using the **badblocks** command for example) a stored in the specified file.
- `-m N4` To specify the percentage of blocks (`N4`) reserved for the system administrator. This is 5% by default.
- `-q` To specify silent execution. This avoids having to redirect the standard output when running the command from a script.
- `-S` To request re-initialization of the superblock and group descriptors. The inode table and the block and inode bitmaps are not modified.
- `-v` To specify verbose execution.

Here is an example of the use of the **mke2fs** command:

```
# mke2fs /dev/hdc3
warning: 103 blocks unused.

Linux ext2 filesystem format
Filesystem label=
22616 inodes, 90113 blocks
4510 blocks (5.00%) reserved for the super user
First data block=1
Block size=1024 (log=0)
Fragment size=1024 (log=0)
11 block groups
8192 blocks per group, 8192 fragments per group
2056 inodes per group
Superblock backups stored on blocks:
    8193, 16385, 24577, 32769, 40961, 49153, 57345,
    65537, 73729, 81921

Writing inode tables: done

Writing superblocks and filesystem accounting
information: done
```

K. Mounting a file system: mount

Before it can be used, a newly created file system must be attached to an existing directory in the file system hierarchy. This directory is called a **mount point** and the operation is called **mounting**. You can **mount** a disk or a file system. It must be noted however, that if any files were contained in the mount point directory before the mounting operation, these files will be inaccessible until the file system is **unmounted**.

1. Listing the mounted file systems: /etc/mtab

The */etc/mtab* file contains the list of the file systems that are currently mounted. This file is maintained by the **mount** and **umount** (unmount) commands.

When called without options or arguments the **mount** command displays the list of file systems currently mounted. When called using the -t **TYPE** option, **mount** displays the currently mounted file systems of the **TYPE** specified.

The following example shows the contents of the */etc/mtab* file and the result of using the **mount** command without options or arguments:

```
[merlin]# cat /etc/mtab
/dev/hdc2 / ext2 rw 0 0
/dev/hdc3 /var ext2 rw 0 0
/dev/hdc4 /tmp ext2 rw 0 0
/dev/sda1 /home ext2 rw,usrquota,grpquota 0 0
none /proc proc rw 0 0
/dev/hdd /cdrom iso9660 ro 0 0
[merlin]# mount
/dev/hdc2 on / type ext2 (rw)
/dev/hdc3 on /var type ext2 (rw)
/dev/hdc4 on /tmp type ext2 (rw)
/dev/sda1 on /home type ext2 (rw,usrquota,grpquota)
none on /proc type proc (rw)
/dev/hdd on /cdrom type iso9660 (ro)
```

2. Mounting a file system manually

To mount a file system manually, use the **mount** command with the following syntax:

```
mount [OPTIONS] SPECIAL_FILE MOUNTING_POINT
```

Here are the main options you can use when mounting a file system:

- `-n` To carry out the mounting operation without updating the /etc/mtab file. This option is necessary when the /etc directory is in a read-only file system (cf. `-r` option).
- `-o` To specify a list of mounting options. In addition you can specify one or more mounting options separated by commas. Here are the principal mounting options:
  - **async**: all input/output to the file system must be carried out asynchronously.
  - **atime**: inode access time must be updated on each access. This is the option by default.
  - **exec**: the execution of binary files is allowed.
  - **noexec**: the execution of binary files is not allowed. This option is useful when the file system contains binaries for other architectures (alpha processor for example).
  - **noatime**: inode access time will not be updated on this file system.
  - **nosuid**: the effect of SUID and GUID bits is inhibited.
  - **ro**: the file system is mounted in read-only mode.
  - **rw**: the file system is mounted in read-write mode.
  - **suid**: the effect of SUID and GUID bits is allowed.
  - **sync**: all input/output operations must be carried out synchronously.

- `-r` to mount the file system in read-only mode (equivalent to `-o ro`).
- `-t` to specify the file system type (following the `-t`). This is not normally necessary as **mount** can generally determine the type automatically. However, this option is useful in the rare cases where **mount** is unable to do this. This will be the case when file system management is to be handled by a module that has not yet been loaded.
- `-w` to mount the file system in read-write mode (equivalent to `-orw`).

When a file system is mounted frequently with the same options on the same mount point, you can describe this operation in the /etc/fstab file. This simplifies the mounting operation, as we shall see in the next section.

3. The /etc/fstab file

This file contains descriptive information on file systems that are used frequently by the operating system. Its role is to allow automatic mounting on system startup. It also simplifies manual mounting: the system administrator does not need to specify the various mounting parameters as **mount** finds them directly in this file.

Thus, once you have described a file system in the /etc/fstab file, all you have to do to mount it is to call the **mount** command specifying the mount point or device concerned. **mount** requires just one of these items in order to identify the corresponding line in the /etc/fstab file.

Structure of the /etc/fstab file

Each file system is described on a separate line of this file. Each line is composed of six fields separated by spaces or tabs:

Field 1   contains the name of the device or the remote file system to be mounted.

Field 2   contains the name of the mount point for the file system. For swap partitions this field must contain the word "**none**".

Field 3   contains the file system type. Here are the types that are most frequently used:

         ext2   for a standard Linux file system,
         msdos   for an MSDOS file system,
         vfat   for a Windows file system,
         iso9660   for a local CD ROM file system,
         nfs   for a remote file system,
         swap   for a swap partition,
         ignore   to prevent the line being taken into account (you can use this for a comments line, for example).

Field 4   contains the list of mount options, separated by commas. The following options may be used (in addition to the options detailed above for the command **mount -o**):

         auto   To indicate that the file system can be mounted automatically.
         noauto   To inhibit automatic mounting of the file system.
         nouser   To ensure that only the system administrator can mount the file system.
         user   To allow the file system to be mounted by any user (this option implies the **noexec**, **nosuid** and **nodev** options).
         sw   To allow automatic activation of the swap partition.

	usrquota	To allow the setting of user quotas.
	grpquota	To allow the setting of group quotas.
Field 5	indicates to the **dump** command that it can dump the file system.	
Field 6	indicates the order in which the file systems are checked by the **fsck** command. A value of 0 (zero) indicates that the file system need not be checked by **fsck**. A value of 1 should be specified for the root file system. Higher values should be used for other file systems. File systems on different drives can be specified with the same value. This is because, **fsck** will start a separate child process for each drive and these processes will work in parallel. In this way the checking phase will be accelerated. Different values should be specified, for file systems on the same drive, as these will be checked sequentially. However, even if the same values are specified, file systems on the same drive will still be checked sequentially. This is because parallel checking by child processes would require more disk head movement and would take longer.	

Here is an example of the /etc/fstab file:

```
/dev/hda3    /                    ext2    defaults    1   1
/dev/hdb1    /usr/local           ext2    defaults    1   1
/dev/hda4    /archives            ext2    defaults    1   1
/dev/hda2    swap                 swap
/dev/hda1    /usr/local/oracle    ext2    defaults    1   1
none         /proc                proc    defaults    1   1
/dev/fd0     /fdmnt               vfat    noauto      0   0
```

4. Mounting file systems automatically

The */etc/fstab* file allows you to mount file systems automatically. You can do this by including the **mount -a** command in one of the initialization scripts (*/etc/rc.d/rc.sysinit* for a Redhat distribution, or */etc/rc.d/rc.S* for a Slackware distribution).

L. Unmounting a file system: umount

To unmount a file system, use the **umount** command. You need indicate only the device or the mount point used by the file system.

The following options can be used with this command:

- `-a` To unmount all the file systems. Generally, this option is used only when the system is stopped so as to ensure that the system is detached safely.
- `-n` To unmount a file system without updating the */etc/mtab* file.
- `-r` To remount a file system in read-only mode if unmounting fails.
- `-t TYPE` To unmount only those file systems of the specified `TYPE`.

It must be noted that a file system cannot be unmounted if any process is currently accessing any of the files it contains. If this is the case, the **fuser** command may be useful.

M. Identifying processes that are using a file system: **fuser**

It may be impossible to unmount a file system because one or more of the files it contains is currently being used:

```
merlin]# umount /home
umount: /home: device is busy
```

In this case you may want to know which files, processes and users are concerned. To find out this information, use the **fuser** command:

```
fuser [OPTIONS] NAME . . .
```

The `NAME` arguments can be files, directories or special files (devices). By default, **fuser** will display the PIDs (Process Identifiers) of any processes using any of the specified arguments (cf. example below). Each of the PIDs is shown with one of the following characters:

    `c` indicating the current/working directory.

    `e` indicating an executable.

    `f` indicating an open file (this character is omitted in default display mode).

    `r` indicating the root directory.

    `m` indicating a shared library.

```
[110]-system(merlin)~:fuser /home/* /home/system/test/*
/home/system:    108c 122c 126c 128c 129c 3332c 3334c   4754c
/home/system/test/see_nice:    5555e
```

The following options can be used:

- `-a` To display all files specified as arguments (by default, only those files accessed by at least one process are shown).
- `-k` To send the SIGKILL signal to all processes that are accessing the files specified as arguments (to send other signals see the `-signal` option below).
- `-i` To ensure that the system will ask for confirmation before sending signals to processes.
- `-l` To display the list of available signals.
- `-m` Specifes that the argument is the name of a file system. It lists all processes accessing files on the specified file system.
- `-n SPACE` To select a name space. The **file** name space is selected by default. The following space values can be specified:
  - **file**   file names
  - **udp**   local UDP ports
  - **tcp**   local TCP ports
- `-s` To specify silent operation. This option saves you having to redirect the output when this command is used either in a script, or by a background process or by **cron**. When this option is specified the `-a`, `-u` and `-v` options are ignored.
- `-signal` To specify a signal other than SIGKILL, which is sent by default (cf. the `-k` option above).
- `-u` To show the user name for each process displayed.
- `-v` (verbose option) to indicate for each process: the user name, the PID, the access type and the process name.

kernel version 2.0 to 2.2

```
[merlin]# fuser
/tmp/tmp:     127c  6011c  6031c
[merlin]# fuser -u /tmp
/tmp:         127c(system)  6011c(root)   6031c(system)
[merlin]# fuser -v /tmp
            USER          PID  ACCESS  COMMAND
/tmp        system        127  ..c..   bash
            root         6011  ..c..   procgr3
            system       6031  ..c..   lab.1
            root       kernel  mount   /tmp
[merlin]# fuser -vm /tmp
            USER          PID  ACCESS  COMMAND
/tmp        sgbd           83  f....   postmaster
            root           99  f....   X
            system        126  f....   GoodStuff
            system        127  c..     bash
            system        128  f....   FvwmPager
            root         6010  e.      proc2
            root         6011  ce.     procgr3
            system       6025  e.      lab.1
            system       6031  ce.     lab.1
```

In the above example, **kernel** appears in the **PID** column, and **mount** appears in the **ACCESS** column. This means that the directory concerned is used by the kernel as a mount point. These indications appear only when the -v option is specified. By default, a file does not appear when it is being used by the kernel alone. However, in this case, **fuser** indicates that there is a certain activity by suggesting you use the -v option:

```
[merlin]# fuser /tmp
 No process references; use -v for the complete list
[merlin]# fuser -v /tmp
            USER         PID ACCESS COMMAND
/tmp        root      kernel mount  /tmp
```

N. Checking and repairing a file system: fsck

In some rare cases, information stored in the superblock may not correspond to the correct file system structure. When this happens, the file system is said to be in a corrupt state. This situation can occur after an abrupt halt of the system which left no time to write the superblock to disk.

In most cases, the **fsck** utility can correct these problems.

Under normal operating conditions, a file system is checked automatically upon system boot after it has been mounted a certain number of times without verification.

In reality, **fsck** is not directly responsible for either checking or repairing the file system. **fsck** merely provides the interface between the system administrator and a set of utilities, each of which is responsible for checking or repairing a particular type of file system:

```
[merlin]# cd /sbin
[merlin]# ls -l *sck*
-rwxr-xr-x   1 root     bin       21864 May 23  1996 dosfsck*
-rwxr-xr-x   2 root     root     251552 Nov 29 15:40 e2fsck*
-rwxr-xr-x   1 root     root       8796 Nov 29 15:40 fsck*
-rwxr-xr-x   2 root     root     251552 Nov 29 15:40 fsck.ext2*
-rwxr-xr-x   1 root     bin       12512 Oct  2  1996 fsck.minix*
-rwxr-xr-x   1 root     bin       22356 May 23  1996 xfsck*
```

Only the general functioning of **fsck** will be described here.

kernel version 2.0 to 2.2

It is advisable to carry out the checking on unmounted file systems in single user mode. Using **fsck** on a mounted file system can damage it beyond repair. **fsck** warns you of this danger:

```
[merlin]# fsck /home
Parallelizing fsck version 1.12 (9-Jul-98)
e2fsck 1.12, 9-Jul-98 for EXT2 FS 0.5b, 95/08/09
/dev/sda1 is mounted.

WARNING!!!  Running e2fsck on a mounted filesystem may cause
SEVERE filesystem damage.

Do you really want to continue (y/n)? no

check aborted.
```

This is because repairs are made on the disk. Any such modifications to a mounted file system will be overwritten by the **sync** command on any subsequent, normal system stoppage.

1. fsck functionality

The **fsck** utility operates in five phases:

Phase 1	checking of inodes, blocks and sizes.
Phase 2	general searching.
Phase 3	searching for any unlinked directories (directories which are not connected with any other item in the file system).
Phase 4	searching for unlinked files, bad blocks, and links pointing to files or directories that no longer exist.
Phase 5	searching for incorrect or unused blocks.

```
[merlin]# fsck /dev/sda1
Parallelizing fsck version 1.12 (9-Jul-98)
e2fsck 1.12, 9-Jul-98 for EXT2 FS 0.5b, 95/08/09
Pass 1      Checking inodes, blocks, and sizes
Pass 2      Checking directory structure
Pass 3      Checking directory connectivity
Pass 4      Checking reference counts
Pass 5      Checking group summary information
/dev/sda1: 23418/133120 files (8.9% non-contiguous)
, 487484/532464 blocks
```

2. **fsck** options

- `-A` checks the file systems referenced in /etc/fstab in one run.
- `-R` when combined with the `-A` option, this option requests that the root file system is skipped.
- `-T` avoids displaying the title on startup.
- `-P` when combined with the `-A` option, this option requests that the root file system is checked in parallel with other file systems.
- `-s` requests that the **fsck** operations are executed in series. This is useful when the various checkers are in interactive mode.
- `-V` activates verbose mode.
- `-t` allows you to specify the type of file system to be checked.
- `-a` requests automatic repair of the file system without any questions being asked. In general, this option is used only when you initialize the file system as it can be dangerous in other circumstances.

O. Swap management

The term swap is used to refer to *swapping* and to *paging*, even though these are different mechanisms.

The swap area can be defined in two ways:
— by a complete partition,
— by a file within a file system.

The first method is the most frequently used. However, the second is more flexible as it allows you to add or remove a swap area on a system as required.

Strictly speaking, a swap area defined by a partition is not a file system. However, as for a file system, it must be mounted on system startup.

1. Setting up a swap area: **mkswap**

First, you have to use the **fdisk** command to create a partition of hex type 82 (LINUX_SWAP). This type is attributed by currently used installation scripts. However, this makes no difference to the Linux kernel as it does not read partition IDs.

Next, you must initialize this partition using the **mkswap** command. This command has the following syntax:

```
mkswap [-c] [-vN] DEVICE [NUMBER_OF_BLOCKS]
```

If the NUMBER_OF_BLOCKS is not specified, **mkswap** calculates it automatically according to page and partition sizes.

In addition, the size of the swap area is rounded-off to an exact number of page sizes.

The `-c` option checks the device for bad blocks. If any bad blocks are found, their number is displayed. It is strongly recommended that this option is used.

The `-vN` option allows you to specify the *style* of the swap area: `-v0` specifies old style, and `-v1` specifies new style. The old style will be chosen by default if the swap area size is not greater than the maximum size of an old style swap area <u>and</u> the kernel version is earlier than 2.1.117.

2. Activating a swap area: **swapon**

A swap area must be activated before it can be used. Although this can be done manually, it is usually done automatically on system startup. First, however, the swap area must be defined in the */etc/fstab* file as follows:

```
/dev/hdc1       none        swap        sw
```

Automatic activation of the swap area is handled by one of the initialization scripts:

— /etc/ec.d/rc.sysinit for a Redhat distribution,
— /etc/ec.d/rc.local for a Slackware distribution.

The **swapon** command is used with one of the following syntaxes:

```
swapon { -a | <specialfile>}
```

When the `-a` option is specified, **swapon** activates all the swap devices listed in the /etc/fstab file. Otherwise, the command activates the swap area associated with the `specialfile` indicated.

Linux can handle up to height swap areas. To optimize performance, it is advisable to attribute them to partitions on different disks and if possible on different controllers. It is also advisable to use the fastest disks with the highest priorities. You can specify the priority of a swap area by adding `,pri=VALUE` to the fourth field of the /etc/fstab file:

```
/dev/hdc1        none         swap        sw,pri=10
```

3. Deactivating a swap area: **swapoff**

The **swapoff** command is used to deactivate the swap area:

```
swapoff { -a | specialfile}
```

When the `-a` option is specified, **swapoff** deactivates all the swap devices listed in the /etc/fstab file. Otherwise, the command deactivates the swap area associated with the `specialfile` indicated.

Chapter 4

User and group management

A. Creating a new account: an overview 73

B. Structure of the /etc/passwd file 75

C. Structure of the /etc/shadow file 77

D. Checking the /etc/passwd and
the /etc/shadow files: **pwck** 78

E. Creating a user account: **useradd** 79
   1. Options for creating a user account 79
   2. Default values used 81

F. Group management 83
   1. Primary groups and secondary groups 83
   2. Management of secondary groups 84
   3. Creating a group: **groupadd** 85
   4. Checking the /etc/group file: **grpck** 86
   5. Modifying group characteristics: **groupmod** .. 86
   6. Deleting a group: **groupdel** 88

G. Modifying a user account: **usermod** 88

H. Deleting an account: **userdel** 89

kernel version 2.0 to 2.2

I.	Configuring user connections: **login**	90
J.	Restricting terminal access	91
	1. Administration access restriction: */etc/securetty* .	91
	2. General access restriction: */etc/usertty*	91
K.	Limiting user resources	93
L.	User information	95
	1. A little history...	95
	2. The */etc/motd* file	96
	3. **news** on Linux	96

Chapter 4

In this chapter, it is assumed that the shadow software suite has been installed on the system.

A Linux user is not necessarily a physical person. A user is merely an entity that can execute a program and can own files on the system. Therefore, a user can be another computing system, system functions, an individual or a group of individuals. Some users exist only in order to own a set of files. The term pseudo-user is often used in this case.

User management is carried out using the following files:
– */etc/passwd*
– */etc/group*
– */etc/shadow*

A. Creating a new account: an overview

Here are the steps involved in creating a new account:
– assign a login name to the user,
– assign the user to a primary group and possibly to secondary groups,
– assign a password to the user,
– define the password's ageing parameters,
– create the user's login (home) directory,
– copy initialization files (*/etc/skel/**) to the user's login directory.

You can carry out this procedure manually by editing the three files /etc/passwd, /etc/group and /etc/shadow. However, this is not recommended for two reasons:

- Any typing errors could make the files unusable and prevent all future logins to the system.
- If you edit the /etc/passwd or the /etc/shadow file while a user is changing password, the latter modification may be lost when you save the file(s).

For these reasons, it is advisable to use the **useradd** command. This command modifies these files properly. This solves the first of these problems. In addition, **useradd** updates these files very selectively in that it acts only on the line concerned. This solves the second problem. Furthermore, **useradd** can create a login directory and copy the necessary initialization files to it.

You can create accounts using the default parameters stored in the /etc/default/useradd file. The contents of this file will be described later.

Before detailing the creation of an account further, we will describe the structure of the /etc/passwd, /etc/group and /etc/shadow files.

B. Structure of the /etc/passwd file

This file is organized by lines. Each line of the file corresponds to a user and is composed of seven fields separated by colons (:). These fields are as follows:

user_name:password:UID:GID:information:home_directory:login_shell

- **user_name**   can contain up to eight characters. The user name is used during the login procedure and for communications between users.
- **password**   can be used to contain the encrypted password. Nowadays, for security reasons, the password is generally contained in the /etc/shadow file. So as not to alter the structure of the /etc/passwd file, the password field remains, but it contains only a star (*).
- **UID**   contains the numerical user ID.
- **GID**   contains the numerical primary group ID for the user.
- **comments**   can contain information that is accessible using utilities such as **finger**. Nowadays, many system administrators prefer to leave this field empty, especially when it can be accessed by the **finger** command from a remote site.
- **home_directory**   contains the name of the user's home directory. The user goes into this directory immediately after logging in.
- **login_shell**   contains the name of the shell program that runs when the user logs in. On Linux systems this is generally **bash** or **tsch**, but you can specify another shell if you wish. In any case, the shell must exist and its name must be present in the /etc/shells file.

Here is an example of the /etc/passwd file:

```
root:x:0:0:root,,,:/root:/bin/bash
bin:x:1:1:bin,,,:/bin:
daemon:x:2:2:daemon,,,:/sbin:
adm:x:3:4:adm,,,:/var/adm:
lp:x:4:7:lp,,,:/var/spool/lpd:
sync:x:5:0:sync,,,:/sbin:/bin/sync
shutdown:x:6:0:shutdown,,,:/sbin:/sbin/shutdown
halt:x:7:0:halt,,,:/sbin:/sbin/haltmail:x:8:12:mail
,,,:/var/spool/mail:
news:x:9:13:news,,,:/usr/lib/news:
uucp:x:10:14:uucp,,,:/var/spool/uucppublic:
operator:x:11:0:operator,,,:/root:/bin/bash
man:x:13:15:man,,,:/usr/man:
postmaster:x:14:12:postmaster,,,:/var/spool/mail:
/bin/bash
ftp:x:404:1:,,,:/home/ftp:/bin/bash
grass:x:503:100:GIS_MAINTENANCE,,,:/home/grass:/bin
/bash
system:x:504:100:system administrator,,,:/home/
system:/bin/bash
nobody:x:65535:100:nobody,,,:/dev/null:
sgbd:x:507:105::/home/sgbd:/bin/sh
webroot:x:1050:110:Web Administrator :/home/webmast
er:/bin/bash webuser:x:1051:110:Web User:/
home/webmaster:/bin/false
squid:x:1052:20:Proxy Administrator:/usr/local/
squid:/bin/bash
calcul:x:1053:20:pri=-5:/home/calcul/bin/bash
```

C. Structure of the /etc/shadow file

This file is organized by lines. Each line of the file corresponds to a user and is composed of eight fields separated by colons (:). These fields are as follows:

Field 1   contains the user (login) name.

Field 2   contains the encrypted password. This can be prefixed by *LK* for a locked account or *RETIRED* for an account that has been deleted.

Field 3   contains the number of days from 01/01/1970 until the last time the password was changed.

Field 4   contains the number of days that must elapse before the password can be changed by the user.

Field 5   contains the number of days that must elapse before the password *must* be changed (expiry date).

Field 6   contains the number of days before the password expiry date, on which the user will be warned of this expiry.

Field 7   contains the number of days after the password expires that must elapse before the account is automatically disabled.

Field 8   contains the number of days from 01/01/1970 until the date on which the account will be automatically disabled.

kernel version 2.0 to 2.2

D. Checking the /etc/passwd and the /etc/shadow files: `pwck`

As mentioned previously in this chapter, it is better not to modify these files directly. This is because any errors in these files could prevent standard utilities from working with them correctly. Furthermore, errors in these files could even prevent any login to the system. In cases where manual intervention is unavoidable, you must verify carefully that no errors have been introduced with your modifications.

The `pwck` command allows you to check the syntax of these files. The following aspects are verified:

- number of fields
- uniqueness of user names
- validity of user and group identifiers
- validity of the primary groups
- validity of the home directories
- validity of the login shells.

`pwck` displays any errors found. If `pwck` detects a line with certain types of error (such as an incorrect format) it offers to delete it for you. If you refuse, `pwck` skips all further checking. If `pwck` finds a line with a duplicated user name, it also prompts you to delete it. However, if you refuse in this case, checking will continue.

By default, this utility checks the /etc/passwd and the /etc/shadow files. You can verify other files by passing their names as arguments. However, these alternative files must have the same structure as /etc/passwd and /etc/shadow respectively. In addition, if you use the -r option, the files are opened in read-only mode and any questions that propose changes are answered **no** automatically.

```
[merlin]# pwck
user news: directory /usr/lib/news does not exist
invalid user name 'postmaster'
user toto: no group 106
user nobody: bad UID (65535)
no matching password file entry
delete line '1053:yYJh7BxohinJ.:10660:0:0:0:7:10660:0'? y
pwck: the files have been updated
```

E. Creating a user account: useradd

The **useradd** command is part of the shadow software suite. It is identical to the **useradd** command of Unix System V, Release 4. This command must be provided with all the characteristics of the account you wish to create. Here is the general syntax to create a new user with this command:

```
useradd    [OPTIONS]    LOGIN_NAME
```

1. Options for creating a user account

Each of these options defines a characteristic of the account to be created:

- `-c COMMENT` — The contents of the comments field in the /etc/passwd file.
- `-d HOME_DIR` — The home (login) directory for the new account. By default, the home directory will be named as the LOGIN_NAME, and created in the default parent home directory (e.g. /home).
- `-e EXPIRE_DATE` — The date on which the user's account will be disabled (specified in MM/DD/YY format).

`-f INACTIVE_DAYS`	The number of days following password expiry that must elapse before the account is disabled. A value of 0 (zero) will disable the account as soon as the password expires. A value of -1 specifies that the account will never be disabled after expiry of the password.
`-g INITIAL_GROUP`	The new user's initial login group (primary group). This can be specified either by its GID or by its group name. The group must be defined in the */etc/group* file.
`-m [-k DIR]`	This option requests the creation of the user's home directory (if it does not already exist). In addition, the files and directories contained in */etc/skel* will be copied to this home directory. Alternatively, the `-k` option allows you to specify a different source directory for these configuration files.
`-s SHELL`	The user's login shell.
`-u UID [-o]`	The UID of the new account. This must be numerical and non negative. It must also be unique unless the `-o` option is specified. By default, the UID is chosen as the smallest value that is greater than 499 and greater than any existing UID.

UID values between 0 and 499 are generally reserved for system accounts.

2. Default values used

In the absence of some of the options defined above, **useradd** uses default values stored in the */etc/default/ useradd* file. Here is an example of this file:

```
# cat /etc/default/useradd
GROUP=100
HOME=/home
INACTIVE=0
EXPIRE=0
SHELL=/bin/bash
SKEL=/etc/skel
```

If this file does not exist, you can create and write it using a text editor. This file simplifies the task of creating a new account. It is especially useful when you want to create several accounts with common characteristics. This file can specify the default value of the following six characteristics that will be used when you create a new account:

GROUP	The primary group GID.
HOME	The parent directory of the home directory (login directory).
INACTIVE	The number of days following password expiry that must elapse before the account is disabled.
EXPIRE	The number of days that must elapse before the password must be changed.
SHELL	The login shell.
SKEL	The directory containing the files to be copied into the new user's home directory.

In the absence of the /etc/default/useradd file, the following default values will be used:

- **GROUP=1**
- **HOME=/home**
- **INACTIVE=-1**
- **EXPIRE=**
- **SHELL=**
- **SKEL=/etc/skel**

To display the command's default values, call **useradd** with the `-D` option, alone. The `-D` option also allows you to modify this file by specifying one or more of the following complementary options:

`-b` DEFAULT_HOME	specifies the default (parent) directory in which a new user's default home directory will be created (the name of this directory will be the login-name).
`-e` EXPIRE_DATE	the date by default on which the user's account will be disabled (MM/DD/YY format).
`-f` INACTIVE_DAYS	the number of days by default after password expiry, that must elapse before the account is disabled.
`-g` INITIAL_GROUP	the default initial login group (primary group). This can be specified by its GID or by its group name. The group must be defined in the /etc/group file.
`-s` SHELL	the user's default login shell.

It must be noted that the /etc/default/useradd file must exist before the options you specify can be taken into account. If this file does not exist you must first create it. This command will not create it for you automatically.

F. Group management

1. Primary groups and secondary groups

Each user is a member of at least one group. This is the user's **primary group** that is defined when the user's account is created.

In addition, the user can be a member of several other **secondary groups**. These are defined in the /etc/group file. In common with the /etc/passwd file, /etc/group is organized by lines. Each line of this file defines a group and is composed of four fields separated by colons:

Field 1   the name of the group (8 characters maximum).
Field 2   the group password (in encrypted format). This field is often left empty, indicating that no password is required.
Field 3   the numerical, unique group identifier (GID).
Field 4   the list of the users who are members of the group. Group members are separated by commas (,).

You are not obliged to update the /etc/group file with groups that are already primary groups. These groups exist already for the system because they appear in the /etc/passwd file.

> Some Unix systems (other than Linux) refuse a login if the user's primary group is not included in /etc/group. For Linux, if a primary group is not included in /etc/group it simply does not have a name. However, this is not necessarily a good approach from an organizational viewpoint.

Here is an example of the /etc/group file:

```
root::0:root,system,squid
bin::1:root,bin,daemon
daemon::2:root,bin,daemon
sys::3:root,bin,adm
adm::4:root,adm,daemon
tty::5:
disk::6:root,adm
lp::7:lp
mem::8:
kmem::9:system
wheel::10:root,system
floppy::11:root,system,webroot
mail::12:mail
news::13:news
uucp::14:uucp,system
man::15:man
operator::16:root,system
games::17:
users::100:games,system
sgbd::105:system
shadow::111:root
nogroup::-2:
web::110:
```

2. Management of secondary groups

Secondary group management techniques vary from one Unix version to another.

Linux has adopted the management style that has been used since BSD 4.2 and System V release 4. With this approach, a user is a member of all the groups for which the user's login name appears in the /etc/group file. The user can use all files belonging to all the groups of which the user is a member (within the limits defined by the group permissions of these files).

This is a very flexible way of sharing files amongst several users without causing security problems (provided that the groups are administrated carefully).

This approach limits the usefulness of the **newgrp** command. On Linux, the main use of this command is to start a new session with a fresh primary group so that each newly created file will belong to this group.

newgrp is part of the Shadow software suite.

Also, if you set the SGID bit on a directory, all new files created in the directory will belong to the same group as the directory. This technique is used on Linux and System V to emulate the default functioning of BSD systems. It adds considerable flexibility to the group mechanism.

3. Creating a group: **groupadd**

The **groupadd** command has the following syntax:

```
groupadd [-g GID [-o]] GROUP_NAME
```

This command creates a new group called `GROUP_NAME`. The `-g` option allows you to specify the GID of the new group. This GID must be unique unless the `-o` option is specified. By default, the GID is chosen as the smallest value that is greater than 499 and greater than any existing GID. Values between 0 and 499 are generally reserved for system accounts.

Linux does not offer a command to change directly the group membership defined in the */etc/group* file. The **useradd** and **usermod** commands (Cf. sections E and G of this chapter) can be used at the individual user level. Indeed, as this is the only automatic solution, it is best to use it if at all possible. However, if you *do* wish to modify group membership directly, your only option is to edit the */etc/group* file manually. As with the */etc/passwd* and */etc/shadow* files, coherence of the */etc/group* file must be carefully checked. To do this, you can use the **grpck** command, as described in the following section.

kernel version 2.0 to 2.2

4. Checking the /etc/group file: **grpck**

This command checks the integrity of the /etc/group file. Each line is checked to have the right format and valid data. The following checks are made:

- that each entry has the correct number of fields,
- that each group name is unique,
- that all group members are defined in the /etc/passwd file.

If any errors are found, **grpck** requests authorization to delete the entry concerned. If you refuse to delete an entry containing a fatal error, no further checking is carried out (**grpck** considers as fatal such errors as the wrong number of fields or a duplicated group name). As with the **pwck** command, you can use the -r option to check the file in read-only mode. Again, in this case any questions that propose changes are answered **no** automatically.

Here is an example of this command:

```
[merlin]# grpck -r
group users: no user games
delete member 'games'? No
grpck: no changes
```

5. Modifying group characteristics: **groupmod**

You can modify a group's name and GID by editing the /etc/group file. However, to avoid any risk of errors that could affect the correct functioning of the system, it is preferable to use the **groupmod** command for this purpose.

```
groupmod [-g GID [-o]] [-n NAME] GROUP_NAME
```

The options can be used as follows:

- `-g GID` to modify the GID of the `GROUP_NAME` group. The indicated value must be unique unless the `-o` option is specified.
- `-n NAME` to change the name of the group from `GROUP_NAME` to `NAME`.

> *You should not modify a group's GID lightly. A new group will be created and files belonging to the old group will not be re-assigned automatically. However, you can reassign these files manually using the following technique:*

```
find . -group 1000 -exec chgrp grp1 {} \;
[merlin]# ls -l fichier_1
-rw-r--r--   1 root     grp1        0 May  4 10:43 fichier_1
[merlin]# ls -ln fichier_1
-rw-r--r--   1 0        1000        0 May  4 10:43 fichier_1
[merlin]# groupmod -g 2000 grp1
[merlin]# ls -l fichier_1
-rw-r--r--   1 root     1000        0 May  4 10:43 fichier_1
[merlin]# find . -group 1000 -exec chgrp grp1 {} \;
[merlin]# ls -l fichier_1
-rw-r--r--   1 root     grp1        0 May  4 10:43 fichier_1
[merlin]# ls -ln fichier_1
-rw-r--r--   1 0        2000        0 May  4 10:43 fichier_1
```

> *The **groupmod** command does not allow you to change the users belonging to a group. This is because group membership is a user characteristic. To add users to a group or to remove them from a group, the **usermod** command should be used for each user concerned (**usermod** is described in section G of this chapter).*

6. Deleting a group: **groupdel**

As with group modification, you can delete a group by editing the /etc/group file. However, for the same security reasons, it is preferable to use the **groupdel** command.

Here is the syntax of this command:

```
groupdel GROUP
```

Having deleted a group, any files or directories belonging to it become "orphans" of the group. To correct this situation, you can either delete these files, or you can re-assign them to another group.

```
[merlin]# ls -l file_1
-rw-r--r--   1 root      grp1      0 May  4 10:43 file_1
[merlin]# groupdel grp1
[merlin]# ls -l file_1
-rw-r--r--   1 root      2000      0 May  4 10:43 file_1
[merlin]# find . -group 2000 -exec chgrp root {} \;
[merlin]# ls -l file_1
-rw-r--r--   1 root      root      0 May  4 10:43 file_1
```

You cannot delete a user's primary group without first deleting the user.

G. Modifying a user account: **usermod**

The **usermod** command allows you to change all user account characteristics except the password, for which the **passwd** command must be used.

The **usermod** command offers the same set of options as **useradd**. In addition, the -l option allows you to modify the login name, provided that the user concerned is not currently logged-in.

LINUX Administration

If at all possible, however, you should avoid modifying a login name. This is because corresponding changes would also need to be carried out for other processes that use the login name, (such as **cron** and the mail system).

In addition, certain precautions must be taken if you modify the UID of the account. Although file user IDs in the user home directory will be changed automatically, any files owned by the user in other directories must be modified manually.

Moreover, you should ensure that the user for whom you wish to modify the UID does not have any processes that are currently running. This is to avoid the UID of such processes becoming invalid. Finally, you must also change the owner of any jobs awaiting execution by **at** and by **cron**.

H. Deleting an account: **userdel**

The **userdel** command is used to delete an account. This command has the following syntax:

```
useradd   [-r]    LOGIN_NAME
```

This command removes all references to the LOGIN_NAME account in the /etc/passwd, /etc/shadow and /etc/group files. In addition, if the -r option is specified, the user's home directory and all its contents will be deleted. However, any files owned by the user in other directories will have to be located and deleted manually. This may be done as follows:

```
find / -user login -exec rm {} \;
```

> *It must be noted that this command will delete directories owned by the user concerned. The files contained in these directories will also be deleted, even if they do not belong to the user concerned.*

This command refuses to delete the account of a user who is currently logged-in.

In addition, you must carry out the following operations when you delete an account:

- delete any of the user's processes that are currently being executed,
- delete the **crontab** for the account,
- delete any jobs awaiting execution (**at**),
- delete any mail messages from the /var/spool/mail/LOGIN_NAME file,
- delete any print jobs.

I. Configuring user connections: `login`

The **login** command is part of the Shadow software suite. It allows you to configure user connections in many different ways. In common with other utilities from the Shadow suite, **login** works closely with the /etc/login.defs file, which it reads each time it is executed.

/etc/login.defs contains many directives. The most important ones are described in this chapter.

J. Restricting terminal access

Linux has two systems that restrict terminal access. The first applies solely to the system administrator and the second applies to all users.

1. Administration access restriction: /etc/securetty

This technique allows you to restrict the terminals that the system administrator can use. This is useful for security reasons. The list of terminals on which the system administrator can log into the system is contained in the /etc/securetty file. It is consulted by the **login** utility. This file is organized with one device name per line (without the /dev/ prefix).

2. General access restriction: /etc/usertty

You can limit the access on some or all of the terminals according to the users concerned and the time when the login request is made. These access restrictions are indicated in the /etc/usertty file.

> This file is used by the login command from the shadow suite.

The /etc/usertty file contains one rule per line. Each rule is made up of three fields separated by colons (:).

The first field contains a list of terminals in the form of special file names without the /dev/ prefix. The star (*) character can be used as a 'wildcard' to indicate all terminals.

The second field contains the list of users to whom the rule applies. As with the terminals field, the * wildcard can be used to specify all users, without the risk of forgetting any of them.

The third field contains a list of time intervals. A time interval is defined by a starting time and a finishing time. These times are indicated in the HHMM format and separated by a dash (-) character. For example, a time interval starting at 8 AM and finishing at 5:30 PM, would be indicated as 0800-1730.

You can limit the effect of a time interval to one or more days using the following prefixes:

Su	Sunday
Mo	Monday
Tu	Tuesday
We	Wednesday
Th	Thursday
Fr	Friday
Sa	Saturday
Wk	Monday to Friday
Al	All days (default value)

Upper case and lower case letters must be respected. If no day prefix is specified, the rule is applied every day.

K. Limiting user resources

Most standard Linux installations allow free access to system resources by default. In this mode, a user can slow down or even block the system, by unlimited consumption of available resources. For example, the user can occupy large areas of memory. The user can also open large numbers of files simultaneously, even to the extent of reaching the maximum number allowed by the system. When this happens no one can open any more files.

An even more serious problem is that a user can also run large numbers of processes, to the extent of reaching the maximum number of executable processes allowed by the system. When this happens, no one can run any more processes.

There are two ways of dealing with this problem, according to the circumstances:
— if the user has a real need for such resources, then the system must be reconfigured in order to optimize its performance,
— if the situation was caused by usage error on the part of a user, measures must be taken to prevent the situation from happening again.

In any case, the necessary steps must be taken to ensure that no user can endanger the correct functioning of the system. To do this, you must limit the resources to which the user has access.

For this purpose, you can use the internal shell command, **ulimit**. This command exists in **bash** and the **Ksh**. However, in this section we will limit our discussion to the **bash ulimit** command (that of the **Ksh** is essentially the same).

kernel version 2.0 to 2.2

You can apply two types of restriction:
- **soft** limits define the use of resources by default when a process is created. A soft limit can be varied.
- **hard** limits define an upper threshold that soft limits cannot exceed.

A user can increase a soft limit up to the value defined by the hard limit.

You can view current limits using the following commands:
- **ulimit -a** displays the current values of soft limits.
- **ulimit -Ha** displays the values of hard limits.

You can specify either soft or hard limits using the following options followed by the limit value:

-c maximum size of a core file.

-d maximum data segment size for a process.

-f maximum size of files created by the shell.

-m maximum amount of physical memory that a process can use.

-s maximum stack size of a process.

-t maximum CPU time that a process can consume (in seconds).

-p maximum size for a pipe (in blocks of 512 bytes).

-n maximum number of open files.

-u maximum number of processes that a user can execute simultaneously.

-v maximum amount of virtual memory that the shell can use.

-S when combined with one of the above options, the -s option specifies a soft limit (this option is used by default).

-H when combined with one of the above options (cdfmstpnuv), the -H option specifies a hard limit.

Modifications apply only to soft limits. Consequently, the only reason to specify -s is to make your command clearer.

Once a hard limit has been set it cannot be increased.

L. User information

1. A little history...

Originally, each branch of Unix had its own user information system. On BSD systems, this consists of displaying the contents of the */etc/motd* file when a user logs in (motd stands for 'message of the day'). It must be noted that a BSD user can deactivate the display of */etc/motd* by creating the *.hushlogin* file in his/her home directory.

On System V, the user information mechanism is more elaborate. It is called **news**. In spite of its name, this system has nothing to do with newsgroups on the Internet. **news** is particular to a system and is independent of any network. It consists of a set of files or items that are placed by authorized users in the */usr/news* directory. Each of these files contains information to be diffused. The name of a file is the title of the information it contains.

The /usr/news directory is generally a link to /var/news.

Users can consult items using the **news** command. When called for the first time this command creates the *.news_time* file in the user's home directory. The time stamp of this file is updated on each subsequent call to **news**. This file ensures that the **news** command displays only those items that have not yet been consulted by the user concerned. The **news** command will be described later in this section.

In common with other Unix systems, you can use both of these user information systems on Linux.

2. The */etc/motd* file

The use of the */etc/motd* file depends on the **login** command. It must be noted that the shadow suite version of this command allows you to activate or deactivate the role of the *.hushlogin* file. You can do this using the HUSHLOGIN directive in the */etc/login.defs* configuration file. This directive must be followed by the name of the file whose presence will inhibit display of the */etc/motd* file. However, it is advisable to use the *.hushlogin* file for this purpose in order to stay coherent with other Unix systems.

3. **news** on Linux

The Linux version of **news** offers the standard options of this command, plus some extra ones.

Before compiling this command, it is advisable to set the NEWDIR variable, in the *Makefile* file, to */var/news* (rather than */var/sysnews*). This is more coherent with standard practice on other Unix systems. In addition, it is advisable to create a symbolic link from */usr/news* to */var/news,* when you install this command. Again, this is for conformity reasons. Also it avoids confusing system administrators, who can come from a wide variety of backgrounds.

Apart from this, the Linux version of the **news** command functions as other versions, with a few useful options added. In particuliar, these options concern the management of items in the /var/news directory.

Here is the general syntax for this command:

```
news [options] [items]
```

When called without options or arguments, the **news** command displays the contents of those items that the user has not yet read (these are the items that are more recent than the *$HOME/.news_time* file). The command then updates the timestamp on the *$HOME/.news_time* file ready for the next call. In practice, this command is rarely called without options or arguments. The `-n` option is often used, which displays the names of current items (without updating the *.news_time* timestamp).

Having consulted the names of current items, you may then decide to read only some of them. To do this, you can specify, the names of the items you want to read as arguments. Again, in this case the *.news_time* timestamp will not be updated.

Here are the standard **news** options:

- `-a` displays all items, whether they have been read or not.
- `-n` displays the names of those items that have not yet been read.
- `-s` displays the number of new items.

Here are some of the supplementary options offered by the Linux version of this command:

- `-d` displays the date of items (in %b %d %Y format, e.g. Jan 14 2000; see the **date** command in the Linux online manual). To be effective, this option must be combined at least with `-n` or `-l`.
- `-Dfmt` is combined with the `-d` option to specify another date format (for the list of format options, see the **strftime**(3) command in the Linux online manual).
- `-f` is used to indicate the directory that contains the news items (other than /var/news).
- `-l` displays item names, one name per line.

This Linux version of **news** also offers the following administration options:

- `-en` deletes those items that are more than n days old (except those specified using the `-x` option or those included in the /var/news/.noexpire file).
- `-xf1,f2,f3...` specifies those items that the `-e` option must not delete. The items to be excluded are separated by commas (,).

These two administration options allow you to clean-up the /var/news directory automatically using the **cron** daemon. This technique is particularly helpful when the **news** system is heavily used.

Chapter 5

Disk management

A. Special file names 100

B. Listing the storage devices 101

kernel version 2.0 to 2.2

A. Special file names

Each storage device on the system has a special file associated with it. The name of the special file generally depends on the interface used to access the device:

— fd*x* for floppy drive interfaces,
— hd*nx* for IDE disk drive interfaces,
— sd*nx* for SCSI disk drive interfaces.

n is a character designating the device according to its connector and to its position on the connector.

For IDE interfaces, *n* can assume the following values:

a	master device on the first IDE connector,
b	slave device on the first IDE connector,
c	master device on the second IDE connector,
d	slave device on the second IDE connector.
...	

x denotes the partition number on the disk. For example, sdb3 identifies the third partition (3) on the second SCSI disk (b).

B. Listing the storage devices

There are several ways of obtaining the list of the peripheral devices on a system. This list is displayed on system startup. However, the **dmesg** command allows you to view this list more comfortably, as and when required:

```
# dmesg
...
hda: QUANTUM FIREBALL_TM1080A, ATA DISK drive
hdc: WDC AC21600H, ATA DISK drive
hdd: MATSHITA CR-583, ATAPI CDROM drive
ide0 at 0x1f0-0x1f7,0x3f6 on irq 14
ide1 at 0x170-0x177,0x376 on irq 15
hda: QUANTUM FIREBALL_TM1080A, 1039MB w/76kB Cache, CHS=528/64/63, DMA
hdc: WDC AC21600H, 1549MB w/128kB Cache, CHS=3148/16/63, DMA
hdd: ATAPI 8X CD-ROM drive, 128kB Cache
...
(scsi0) Adaptec AHA-294X Ultra SCSI host adapter found at PCI 9/0
(scsi0) Narrow Channel, SCSI ID=7, 16/255 SCBs
(scsi0) Downloading sequencer code... 419 instructions downloaded
scsi0 : Adaptec AHA274x/284x/294x (EISA/VLB/PCI-Fast SCSI)
  5.1.10/3.2.4
       Adaptec AHA-294X Ultra SCSI host adapter
scsi : 1 host.
  Vendor: QUANTUM    Model: FIREBALL540S    Rev: 1Q08
  Type:   Direct-Access                 ANSI SCSI revision: 02
Detected scsi disk sda at scsi0, channel 0, id 1, lun 0
(scsi0:0:1:0) Synchronous at 10.0 Mbyte/sec, offset 8.
scsi : detected 1 SCSI disk total.
SCSI device sda: hdwr sector= 512 bytes. Sectors= 1065235
[520 MB] [0.5 GB]
...
Partition check:
 sda: sda1
 hda: hda1 hda2
 hdc: hdc1 hdc2 hdc3 hdc4
```

A great deal of information is supplied by this command, most of which you may not require for everyday use.

A quicker way to obtain key storage device information is to view the contents of the /proc/partitions file. This file has been available since version 2.2.0 of the Linux kernel.

```
[3]-system(merlin)~:cat /proc/partitions
major minor   #blocks   name

    8     0    532617  sda
    8     1    532464  sda1
    3     0   1064448  hda
    3     1    820480  hda1
    3     2    243936  hda2
   22     0   1586592  hdc
   22     1     33232  hdc1
   22     2   1433880  hdc2
   22     3     90216  hdc3
   22     4     29232  hdc4
   22    64    260448  hdd
```

The /proc/partitions file contains the name and partitions of each on-line device. For each item, the major and minor number of the special file is supplied along with the number of blocks that it contains.

Chapter 6

Archiving and restoring

- **A. Archiving strategies** 105

- **B. Archiving and restoring utilities: dump and restore** 106
    1. **dump** 107
    2. **restore** 109

- **C. The tar command** 111
    1. Function modes 112
    2. General options 112

- **D. The cpio command** 113
    1. Creating a cpio archive 114
    2. Viewing the contents of a **cpio** archive 117
    3. Extracting files from a **cpio** archive 118

- **E. tar versus cpio** 120

- **F. The dd command** 121

- **G. Tape management** 125
    1. Names of special files for tape devices 125
    2. Handling tapes: **mt** 127

kernel version 2.0 to 2.2

H. Remote archiving and restoring **130**

1. Archiving local files on a remote tape device . . **130**
2. Archiving remote files on the local tape device . **131**
3. Restoring a remote archive on to your local site **131**
4. Restoring a local archive on to a remote site . . **131**

Chapter 6

Several archiving and restoring tools are available on Linux. In this chapter, we will cover the standard utilities that are present on most Unix systems. These utilities are either already included in Linux distributions, or shortly will be.

These standard tools are:
- **dump** and **restore**
- **tar**
- **cpio**
- **dd**.

> *The Linux versions of **dump** and **restore** are still in development. Consequently, they are not yet included in Linux distributions and must be installed separately.*

A. Archiving strategies

If you do not have very large volumes of data to back up, you can archive all of it systematically.

However, the more data you have to save, the more time you will need to back it up. This means that you will archive less frequently and you will be less able to ensure a "worst-case" restoration in a reasonably up-to-date state.

kernel version 2.0 to 2.2

One objective of an archiving strategy is to minimize the loss of working time in the event of data being lost. The working time you stand to lose is made up of two components:

- the working time lost up to the moment the data restoration would begin (this time cannot be less than the archiving time),
- the time required to restore the data.

Thus, in the event of a problem, the loss of working time is the sum of the following elements:

- the time required to archive the data,
- the time elapsed since the last archive was completed,
- the time required to restore the data.

B. Archiving and restoring utilities: dump and restore

These are the oldest Unix archiving and restoring utilities. They originally appeared with AT&T Unix version 6, and were subsequently improved with BSD versions (notably BSD 4.2 for restore).

These functions are currently being developed for Linux. However, available versions seem already very stable, even though version 1.0 has not yet been released.

Originally, these utilities were used to archive and restore entire partitions. However, they now allow you to work at directory level.

Unlike most Unix commands, the options for these utilities are not prefixed with a dash (-), although Linux versions leave you the choice of using a dash or not.

In all cases, the files and directories are archived *physically* with their inode numbers. Where possible they will be restored with the same inode numbers, even though this technique can result in a corrupted file system.

1. dump

The **dump** utility allows you to archive all or part of a partition. First however, you must check the integrity of the partition concerned. Also, you are strongly advised to unmount this partition. If you do not do this you may produce an unusable archive.

It is not advisable to carry out multi-volume archiving with the current version of **dump** (0.3).

dump options

- `0-9` indicates the **dump** level. Level 0 backs up the entire file system. Higher levels will back-up all files modified since the last lower-level dump.
- `u` (if **dump** is successful) updates the */etc/dumpdates* file with a record containing three fields:
  - name of the file system (or name of the special file associated with the partition)
  - dump level
  - back-up timestamp.
- `f` is followed by the name of the regular or special file to which the archive must be written. By default a tape device (*/dev/rmt8*) is used. If the file name is specified as '-' dump writes to the standard output. This allows you to use **dump** in a pipeline.

n specifies that all users who are members of the **operator** group will be notified should **dump** require operator intervention. This will be done using a command such as **wall**.

dump backup procedure

The **dump** command makes an asynchronous backup. The original process spawns a supervisor process which in turn spawns three other processes. These last processes carry-out the reading and writing operations.

```
merlin]# dump 0f /root/dump.out /dev/sda1 /root/dump.log 2&1 &
[1] 1750
[merlin]# ps aujx|egrep "PID|dump"|grep -v egrep
ps ajx|egrep "PID|dump"|grep -v egrep
 PPID   PID  PGID   SID TTY      TPGID STAT  UID   TIME COMMAND
 4859  5143  5143  4098 ttyp2     5143 S     0    0:01 dump 0f /root/dump.out
/dev/sda1
 5143  5145  5143  4098 ttyp2     5143 D     0    0:04 dump 0f /root/dump.out
/dev/sda1
 5145  5146  5143  4098 ttyp2     5143 S     0    0:07 dump 0f /root/dump.out
/dev/sda1
 5145  5147  5143  4098 ttyp2     5143 S     0    0:07 dump 0f /root/dump.out
/dev/sda1
 5145  5148  5143  4098 ttyp2     5143 S     0    0:07 dump 0f /root/dump.out
/dev/sda1
[merlin]# dump 0uf - /dev/sda1|dd of=/dev/sdb2
  DUMP: Date of this level 0 dump: Mon May  3 20:56:31 1999
  DUMP: Date of last level 0 dump: the epoch
  DUMP: Dumping /dev/sda1 (/home) to standard output
  DUMP: mapping (Pass I) [regular files]
  DUMP: mapping (Pass II) [directories]
  DUMP: estimated 487138 tape blocks.
  DUMP: dumping (Pass III) [directories]
  DUMP: dumping (Pass IV) [regular files]
  DUMP: DUMP: 487839 tape blocks
  DUMP: level 0 dump on Mon May  3 20:56:31 1999
  DUMP: DUMP IS DONE
975660+0 records in
975660+0 records out
```

the /etc/dumpdates file

This file contains the system archive history. As detailed above, you can update this file after each successful backup, by specifying the u option when you call the **dump** command.

```
[merlin]# cat /etc/dumpdates
/dev/hdc2         0 Fri Dec 11 21:03:35 1998
/dev/sda1         0 Mon May  3 20:56:31 1999
```

2. restore

The **restore** utility allows you to list the contents of an archive. It also allows you to make a complete or partial restore.

Here is the syntax of the **restore** command:

```
restore    [OPTIONS]    [FILE(S)]
```

The following options can be used with this command:

- b   To specify the block size of the archive tape (in kilobytes). If this is not specified, **restore** will try to determine it dynamically.
- h   To extract only the directories and not the files referenced (avoiding restoration of complete subtrees).
- i   To open an interactive session. Here are the commands you can use in this mode:
    - **add**   Followed by the names of files and directories to be added to the extraction list. If no argument is specified the current directory is added.
    - **cd**   Followed by the name of the new current directory.

kernel version 2.0 to 2.2

delete	Followed by the names of files and directories to be deleted from the extraction list. If no argument is specified the current directory is deleted.
extract	Extracts the files and directories on the extraction list.
help	Displays a summary of available commands.
ls	Lists the specified directory. If no argument is given the current directory is listed.
pwd	Displays the full path of the current directory.
quit	Leaves **restore**.
setmodes	Specifies that the owner, permissions and times for all the files and directories on the extraction list must be restored identically to the originals.
verbose	Has a toggle action. When set it causes the **ls** command to list inodes and **restore** to display information on extracted files.

- `r` To restore the whole tape.
- `R` To resume restoring from a specified tape from a multi-tape archive. This is not necessarily the first tape of the set. This allows you to resume an archive after it has been interrupted.
- `s n` To restore dump file number n from a tape containing several dump files.
- `t` To check the presence of specified files. If no arguments are specified, this option lists the contents of the archive.
- `x` To extract the specified files from the archive. If no files are specified, the whole file system is extracted.

- f To indicate the name of the regular or special file containing the archive. By default the /dev/rmt8 tape device is used. If the file name is specified as '-', **restore** reads from the standard input. This allows you to use it in a pipeline.
- v To specify verbose mode. In this mode the type and name of each file appears as it is extracted (by default the **restore** command operates silently).
- y When you specify this option **restore** will try to skip any bad blocks it finds in the archive and continue restoring (by default, if **restore** encounters any tape errors it asks the operator whether it should abort or not).

C. The tar command

tar, which stands for *tape archive*, is a very old Unix command. Although its principal role was to archive a file hierarchy to tape, this command can now archive to any regular or special file (not necessarily a tape). In all cases, the file to which **tar** archives is called a **tarfile**.

Unlike the **dump** and **restore** commands, **tar** can be used to archive, to display contents of an archive or to restore an archive. In addition, **tar** offers a number of complementary functions.

Here is the general syntax for the **tar** command:

```
tar   MODE   [OPTIONS]   FILE(S) and/or
DIRECTORY(IES)
```

kernel version 2.0 to 2.2

1. Function modes

One of the following function **modes** must be chosen:

- `A` To append an archive to another archive.
- `c` To create a new archive.
- `d` To find the differences between an archive and a file system.
- `r` To append one or more files/directories to an archive.
- `t` To list the contents of an archive.
- `u` To append specified files to an archive, only if they are more recent than those already stored in the archive.
- `x` To extract all or part of an archive.

2. General options

The main general options are as follows:

- `b n` To specify the block size in units of 512 bytes (by default, n=20).
- `f` To specify a regular or special file. This is /dev/rmt0 by default. You can define a different default file by using the TAPE environment variable. In this way you can avoid using the `f` option. You can indicate a remote file using the site:file format.
- `v` To specify verbose functioning. In this mode the names of processed files are listed. Unlike some **tar** versions, the Linux `v` option uses the standard error instead of the standard output. This avoids problems when using commands such as the following one:

```
$ tar cvf FILE(S) | gzip > arc.z
```

- w To stipulate that **tar** must request confirmation for each action before carrying it out.
- z To pipe the archive through the **gzip** compression utility.
- Z To pipe the archive through the **compress** compression utility.

D. The `cpio` command

cpio can be used to archive, to display the contents of an archive or to restore an archive. In addition to restoring archives that it has produced itself, **cpio** can restore archives produced by **tar**. It was introduced with System V to replace **tar** (although the latter is still widely used).

In common with **tar**, the **cpio** command creates archives that are totally independent of the file systems concerned. This allows you to restore them onto another system.

cpio has three functioning modes, of which you must choose one. Each functioning mode is indicated by a different option:

- `-o` (copy-out mode) creates an archive. The names of the files to be archived are supplied on the standard input and the result is written to the standard output.
- `-i` (copy-in mode) either extracts files from an archive or lists the contents of an archive. You can specify the list of files to be extracted on the standard input. Alternatively, you can supply the name of an archive to be listed, again on the standard input.

-p (copy-pass mode) combines copy-out and copy-in mode. Files specified on the standard input are transferred to the directory specified in the command line given after this option.

In all cases, **cpio** functions with its standard input and standard output streams. This functionality makes it very convenient to combine **cpio** with other commands. For example, you can use **find** to select the files you want to archive.

If you wish to use **cpio** with other commands, you may need to use redirections. As the standard input and output are already being used, **cpio** transmits messages on the standard error. You must remember this if you want to redirect these messages to a file for future reference.

1. Creating a cpio archive

You can create an archive by using **cpio** in copy-out mode (`cpio -o`). The names of the files to be archived must be supplied on the standard input.

For example, you can archive the files from the **dir** directory using the following pipeline:

```
$ ls dir | cpio -o > archive
```

As the `ls dir` command will list the files specifically contained in `dir`, this pipeline will work, only if both of the following conditions are satisfied:

- that `dir` is the current directory of the command and,
- that either `dir` is specified as an absolute path, or that `dir` is not specified at all (calling **ls** without an argument).

Alternatively, you can modify this command so that it will work whether `dir` is the current directory of the command or not (again `dir` must be specified as an absolute path):

```
$ ls dir | (cd dir ; cpio -o > archive)
```

or

```
$ cd dir ; ls | cpio -o > archive
```

However, you must be careful not to create the archive file in the current directory (`dir`) as this will result in the archive file being archived as well.

There are two ways of avoiding these difficulties:

— You can connect **cpio** to the **find** command instead of the **ls** command. The advantage of using the **find** command is that it lists complete path names.

```
$ find dir -type f -print| cpio -o > archive
```

— You can create a file containing the names of the files you want to archive, with one file name per line. Then, you can use the following pipeline (where `list` is the file you created):

```
$ cat list | cpio -o > archive
```

In addition, you can combine these methods. For example, you can use the following pipeline to archive those files contained in dir that have been modified in the last 24 hours (N.B. the list file must already exist):

```
$ find dir -type f -mtime -1 -print  list; cat
list | cpio -o > archive
```

The following example is a simple script that archives the files listed in the *archive.list* file (with one file name per line):

```
#!/bin/sh
if [ ! -r archive.list ];then
echo "`basename $0`: problem with archive.list !"
exit 1
fi
if [ $# -ne 1 ];then
echo "`basename $0`: file by default : /dev/fd0"
set /dev/fd0
fi
if [ ! -w "$1" ];then
echo "`basename $0`: cannot write to $1 file"
exit 1
fi
cat archive.list | cpio -ov > $1
```

You can use a number of options with copy-in mode:

- `-a` So as not to modify the inode of the files concerned. This makes it look as if the files have not just been read. For this option to be effective you must either be root, or the owner of the archived files (or both).
- `-B` To set the block size to 5120 bytes, instead of 512 bytes (the default value).
- `-c` To create an archive in ASCII format. This makes the archive more portable. However, you must not use this format with a file system that has more than 65536 inodes.
- `-L` To copy the files pointed to by any symbolic links, rather than copying the symbolic links themselves (by default the symbolic links are archived and not the files to which they point).
- `-v` (verbose option) to list the names of the files that are processed.

In addition to these relatively standard options, the GNU version of **cpio** offers other options. Here are two of them:

-O To specify an archive file name to be used instead of the standard output. This saves you redirecting the standard output.

-A To append files to an existing archive.

> *Some versions of **cpio** conform to the XPG4 or POSIX.2 specifications and do not allow you to archive more than 2 Gbytes of data. Consequently, if you wish to be compliant with these versions, the data you archive must not exceed this size limit. You can always compress the data first, of course.*

2. Viewing the contents of a **cpio** archive

You can view a **cpio** archive in two ways:

```
$ cpio -it   <ARCHIVE_FILE
```

This command lists the archive contents in an format similar to that produced by the **ls -1** command:

```
[70]-system(merlin)~:cpio -it < arc
nmap
nmap-1
nmap-2
plan_util
procinfo
rpc
sher.html
tests/
34 blocks
```

```
$ cpio -itv <+ARCHIVE_FILE
```

This command lists the archive contents in an format similar to that produced by the **ls -1** command:

```
[71]-system(merlin)~:cpio -itv < arc
-rw-------   1 system   users         0 Mar 19 13:15 nmap
-rw-------   1 system   users      2834 Mar 19 13:16 nmap-1
-rw-------   1 system   users      5647 Mar 19 13:19 nmap-2
-rw-------   1 system   users       856 Apr 19 16:25 plan_util
-rw-------   1 system   users      1213 Feb 15 09:33 procinfo
-rw-------   1 system   users       819 Apr  2 17:16 rpc
-rw-------   1 system   users      5691 Nov 19 20:37 sher.html
drwx------   2 system   users         0 Apr 15 13:17 tests/
34 blocks
```

3. Extracting files from a **cpio** archive

File extraction is also done in copy-in mode. In this mode **cpio** processes the data it reads on its standard input. To enable **cpio** to process the contents of a file, you must transmit them to this command using a redirection or a pipe.

By default, the entire contents of the archive is restored. **cpio** also allows you to restore certain files only from an archive. Indeed, the range of partial restore options offered by **cpio** is greater than that offered by **tar**.

You have a choice of over 20 options when extracting files from a **cpio** archive. Here is a selection of those most commonly used:

-b To inverse the order of each pair of bytes (in each half-word) and of each pair of half-words (in each word). This option provides for different data formats used for 32 bit integers (by bigendian / littleendian machines).

-s To inverse the order of each pair of bytes (in each half-word).

-S To inverse the order of each pair of half-words (in each word).

-B To set the block size to 5120 bytes, instead of 512 bytes (the default value).
-c To create an archive in ASCII format. This is an old format, but a portable one.
-d To request that directories are created where they are required and they do not exist already.
-H To indicate one of the following formats:

    bin Binary format. This option is useful to restore old files stored in this format, which is now obsolete.

    odc The old POSIX.1 portable format.

    newc The new System V R4 portable format. This format supports file systems having more than 65536 inodes.

    crc The new System V R4 portable format including a checksum.

    tar The old **tar** format.

    ustar The POSIX.1 **tar** format.

    hpbin The old (obsolete) format used by HPUX systems.

    hpodc The portable format used by HPUX systems.

-L To copy the files pointed to by any symbolic links rather than copying the symbolic links themselves.
-m To keep the last modification times of the files stored in the archive, instead of updating them with the current time.
-r To modify the name of each file extracted, interactively.

`-R [user]`
`[:.][group]` To modify the owner and/or the group of the extracted files. You must specify either a user or a group. If you include a **:** or **.** separator, but do not specify a group, then the files are assigned to the login group of the specified user.

`-u` To replace all files without the system requesting confirmation (in the case of overwriting a more recent version).

`-v` (verbose option) to list the names of the files that are processed.

E. `tar` versus `cpio`

The **cpio** command has several advantages over **tar**:

- **cpio** can be used to make a multi-volume archive. Although the standard version of **tar** does not support this function, the GNU version does. However, using the GNU version of **tar** for this purpose is not advisable as the archive you produce will be less portable.
- **cpio** writes archive data in a more efficient way, making better use of the available space.
- **cpio** ignores any bad blocks and continues processing (if **tar** finds any bad blocks it fails).
- **cpio** will archive any type of file (**tar** is more specialized in file hierarchies).
- When **tar** extracts a single file, it reconstitutes the hierarchy included in the file name. This is generally not required for a single file. In this case you can use **cpio** to extract the file, and possibly rename it. **cpio** recognizes the **tar** format, and will restore the file without re-creating the hierarchy.

On the other hand, **tar** has the following advantages over **cpio**:

- **tar** allows you to specify any block size you want, as a multiple of 512 bytes. With the standard **cpio** version you can choose from only two values: 512 bytes or 5120 bytes. On the other hand, the GNU version of **cpio** does allow you to choose different block sizes using the blocksize=VALUE option. However archives produced using this option will have restricted portability as long as the other versions of **cpio** do not share this functionality.
- **tar** allows you to compress or decompress an archive directly by specifying the -z or the -Z options (resulting in automatic calls being made to **gzip/ungzip** or **compress/uncompress** respectively).

Finally, it is preferable to use **dump** if you do not know the maximum length of the path names of the files that you want to archive. This is because **tar** and **cpio** do not allow path names longer than 100 and 128 characters respectively.

F. The dd command

This command is not specifically designed to work with archives. Essentially, it is a file conversion and formatting utility. However, as we shall see, it is very useful for many purposes, particularly for remote archiving and restoring.

The command first appeared with Unix version 7. Today, **dd** is present on all Unix systems.

In its simplest mode, **dd** simply copies its standard input to its standard output. However, this utility can do much more than that.

Here is the syntax of this command:

`dd [OPTION=VALUE]`

Unlike most Unix commands, the **dd** options are not prefixed with a dash (-). Each option is assigned a value using an equals sign (=).

Here is a list of these options:

- `if` To specify the input file. If this option is absent, the standard input is used.
- `of` To specify the output file. If this option is absent, the standard output is used.
- `ibs` To specify the block size used to read in. By default, the input block size is 512 bytes.
- `obs` To specify the block size used to write out. By default, the output block size is 512 bytes.
- `bs` To specify the block size used to read and to write. This avoids using `ibs` and `obs` to specify the same value.
- `cbs` To specify the block size used for conversion.
- `skip` To skip the specified number of blocks at the beginning of the input. The block size is that specified by `ibs` or `bs` (or 512 bytes by default).
- `seek` To skip the specified number of blocks at the beginning of the output. The block size is that specified by `obs` or `bs` (or 512 bytes by default).
- `conv` To indicate how you want to convert the data. You can specify a list of keywords separated with commas (,). Here are the keywords you can use:
  - **ascii** To convert from EBCDIC to ASCII.
  - **ebcdic** To convert from ASCII to EBCDIC.

ibm	To convert from ASCII to IBM type EBCDIC.
block	To pad-out records that are terminated with a newline. The newline is replaced with spaces to pad the record out to the block size indicated by the `cbs` option (or to 512 bytes by default).
unblock	To replace trailing spaces in block sized records with a newline (the opposite of the block function).
lcase	To convert from upper-case to lower-case.
ucase	To convert from lower-case to upper-case.
swap	To swap over every pair of bytes read.
noerror	To specify that the process must continue after read errors (by default the command stops if it finds any error).
notrunc	To specify that the output must not be truncated in the case of blocks greater than the block size indicated by the `ibs` option.
sync	To padout input blocks with NULL characters up to the block size indicated by the `ibs` option.

> *You can choose from a number of units when indicating size values for* `ibs`, `obs`, `bs` *and* `cbs`. *You can use one of the following suffixes:*
>
> – *k for kilobytes*
> – *b for block units of 512 bytes*
> – *c for bytes*
> – *w for word units of 2 bytes*
> – *xm for units of m bytes.*

For example a size of 5120 bytes for `bs` can be indicated in any of the following ways:

`bs=5k, bs=10b, bs=5120c, bs=2560w or bs=10x512`

When the **dd** command has finished processing, it indicates the numbers of full and partially filled records it has read, and the numbers of full and partially filled records it has written.

G. Tape management

1. Names of special files for tape devices

Linux handles many different types of tape device. The special file name depends largely on the type of interface used: SCSI, IDE QIC-02, parallel or floppy.

For SCSI devices, the following special file names are used:

Special file	Device
/dev/nst[031]	SCSI device, mode 0, rewindable
/dev/nst[031]	SCSI device, mode 0, non-rewindable
/dev/nst[031]l	SCSI device, mode 1, rewindable
/dev/nst[031]l	SCSI device, mode 1, non-rewindable
/dev/nst[031]m	SCSI device, mode 2, rewindable
/dev/nst[031]m	SCSI device, mode 2, non-rewindable
/dev/nst[031]a	SCSI device, mode 3, rewindable
/dev/nst[031]a	SCSI device, mode 3, non-rewindable

For the IDE bus, only one tape device is supported at present:

Special file	Device
/dev/ht0	rewindable tape device
/dev/nht0	non-rewindable tape device

kernel version 2.0 to 2.2

The QIC-02 interface is used for tape devices with the following formats: QIC11, QIC24, QIC120 and QIC150. The essential differences in these formats concern the numbers of tracks and storage densities. The special file used depends on the format in each case:

Format	Special file	Device	Tracks
QIC-11	/dev/tpqic11	rewindable	4
	/dev/ntpqic11	non-rewindable	
QIC-24	/dev/tpqic24	rewindable	9
	/dev/ntpqic24	non-rewindable	
QIC-120	/dev/tpqic120	rewindable	15
	/dev/ntpqic120	non-rewindable	
QIC-150	/dev/tpqic150	rewindable	18
	/dev/ntpqic150	non-rewindable	

You can also connect up to four tape devices on parallel ports. These devices use the following special files:

Special file	Device
/dev/pt[0-3]	rewindable tape device
/dev/npt[0-3]	non-rewindable tape device

A further possibility is to install a tape device onto a floppy disk drive controller. This is certainly the most economical solution. You can do this with tape formats QIC40, QIC80 or QIC117. The following special files are used:

Special file	Device
/dev/qft[0-3]	rewindable
/dev/nqft[0-3]	non-rewindable
/dev/zqft[0-3]	rewindable, compression
/dev/nzqft[0-3]	non-rewindable, compression
/dev/rawqft[0-3]	rewindable, without end-of-file marker
/dev/nrawqft[0-3]	no- rewindable, without end-of-file marker

As you probably have only one tape device connected to your system, you may wish to create a link from /dev/tape to the special file associated with it. This is a useful because /dev/tape is the default name used by commands such as **mt**. Another useful technique is to define the TAPE environment variable with the name of the special file associated with your tape device. This variable is used by utilities such as **tar** and **mt**.

2. Handling tapes: mt

The **mt** utility is part of the GNU **cpio** software suite. It allows you to handle tape devices. It can be used only with tape drives and not with other device types.

Here is the syntax for this command:

```
mt [-f DEVICE] OPERATION
```

You can specify the device concerned in three ways:
- If you do not indicate a device, **mt** uses the /dev/tape device. This default device is defined in the /usr/include/sys/mtio.h file. It must be noted that /dev/tape is usually a link to a real, special file.
- You can store the name of the special file concerned in the TAPE environment variable. If defined, this variable has priority over the device by default.
- You can specify the -f option followed by the name of the special file concerned. This technique has priority over the two previous ones described above.

If your system is on a TCP/IP network, you can indicate a device on a remote machine. To do this you must declare the remote machine in either the /etc/hosts.equiv file or a .rhosts file. In addition, you must prefix the name of the special file by **HOST:**, where HOST is the name or the IP address of the remote system.

The operation you wish to carry out on the tape is indicated using a keyword. You can abbreviate the keyword as long as the abbreviation is unambiguous. Some keywords can be followed by a number to indicate how many times you want the operation to be carried out. If no number is indicated, the operation concerned will be executed just once. Here is the list of keywords you can use. The notation [n] indicates that a number may be specified. The default value for n is 1:

      `eof [n]`   To write n EOF markers at the current position on the tape.

     `weof [n]`   This has the same action as `eof [n]`.

      `fsf [n]`   To move forwards to the beginning of the nth file further on.

      `bsf [n]`   To move backwards to the beginning of the nth file further back.

      `fsr [n]`   To move forwards by n blocks.

      `bsr [n]`   To move backwards by n blocks.

`asf [n]`	To go to the beginning of the nth file on the tape. This is the equivalent of `rewind` followed by `fsf n`.
`seek [n]`	To go to the beginning of the nth block from the beginning of the tape.
`eom`	To move to the end of the last record on the tape. This is used to add records to the end of a tape.
`rewind`	To rewind to the beginning of the tape.
`offline`	To rewind the tape, and, if possible, unload the tape or switch the device offline.
`rewoffl`	This has the same action as `offline`.
`status`	To display information on the status of the device.
`retension`	To "re-tension" the tape. This is done by rewinding to the beginning of the tape, then winding to the end of the tape and then rewinding again to the beginning of the tape.
`erase`	To erase the contents of the tape.

H. Remote archiving and restoring

In this section we will describe how you can use a TCP/IP network to centralize the archiving and restoring of data. This technique allows one tape device to be used by several sites, with the tape device concerned being connected to a machine dedicated to this purpose. We will cover this topic, without entering into the details of installing and configuring such a network.

Several combinations can be implemented using either **tar** or **cpio**.

- archiving local files on a remote tape device,
- archiving remote files on the local tape device,
- restoring a remote archive on to your local site,
- restoring a local archive on to a remote site.

These operations are possible, thanks to the Berkeley **rsh** (remote shell) command. This command allows you to carry out actions on remote sites (provided that the /etc/hosts.equiv or ~/.rhosts file contain the necessary information).

1. Archiving local files on a remote tape device

Using tar
```
tar cvf - files | rsh host "dd of=archive_file"
```

Using cpio
```
ls files | cpio -o | rsh host "dd of=archive_file"
```

2. **Archiving remote files on the local tape device**

Using tar
rsh *host* tar cf - *files* | dd of=*archive_file*

Using cpio
rsh *host* "ls *files* | cpio -o" | dd of=*archive_file*

3. **Restoring a remote archive on to your local site**

Using tar
rsh *host* dd if=*archive_file* | tar xf -

Using cpio
rsh *host* dd if=*archive_file* | cpio -i

4. **Restoring a local archive on to a remote site**

Using tar
dd if=*archive_file* | rsh *host* tar xf -

Using cpio
dd if=*archive_file* | rsh *host* cpio -i

personal notes

Chapter 7

Resource management

- **A. Monitoring system activity: uptime, w** **135**
    1. The **uptime** command 135
    2. The **w** command 136
- **B. Process management** **137**
    1. The process concept 137
    2. Spawning processes 137
    3. Process groups 139
    4. Process states 139
    5. Scheduling 141
    6. The top command 146
    7. Sending signals to processes:
       kill, killall, killall5 147
- **C. Monitoring the memory and the CPU: vmstat** **148**
- **D. Disk space monitoring** **151**
    1. The **df** command 151
    2. The **du** command 154
- **E. Monitoring the swap: swapon, free** **157**

kernel version 2.0 to 2.2

Once it is running, the system must check that all users can access resources correctly according to the permissions that have been assigned. The system checks this continually. As a basic principle, a system that allows non-exclusive access to resources must ensure that no user blocks any resource.

If the system is running slowly, you may wish to find out the bottleneck that is causing this situation. A bottleneck can be a resource that a number of processes are trying to access at once. It can also be a resource with insufficient capacity such as a disk that operates too slowly.

The following items must be monitored:
- CPU
- memory
- disk partitions
- printers.

Most of the commands described in this chapter come from the procps-1.01 software suite. Unlike most other commands, those from this suite are specific to Linux. They access system tables contained in the /proc file system.

A. Monitoring system activity: uptime, w

1. The uptime command

This command originated from BSD systems. It gives some basic information on how the system is running:

```
# uptime
10:04 am up 21 min, 3 users, load average: 0.11, 0.05, 0.08
```

This command provides the following information:
— current time,
— how long the system has been running,
— how many users are logged-in,
— system load averages for the last 1, 5 and 15 minutes.

It must be noted that the load information is given with respect to specific time intervals. System loading levels are not necessarily related to system response time. A system can be heavily loaded and still have quick response times. Conversely, a lightly loaded system may have slow response times. A large number of small processes may result in high loads without disrupting the system unduly. On the other hand, a single large process may slow down the system considerably.

kernel version 2.0 to 2.2

2. The w command

This command shows the same information as **uptime** plus a report summarizing the activity of the system users:

```
[72]-system(merlin)~:w
1:04pm   up 3 days, 14:29,   4 users,   load average: 0.00, 0.00, 0.00
USER     TTY    FROM            LOGIN@     IDLE   JCPU   PCPU   WHAT
system   ttyp0  :0.0            Fri10pm    1:53m  6.70s  ?      -
system   ttyp1  :0.0            Fri10pm    1:56m  1.01s  0.36s  -su
system   ttyp2  arthur.dorset.  10:12am    0.00s  0.58s  0.09s  w
system   ttyp3  :0.0            10:45am    1:55m  0.31s  0.03s  vi
```

The following information is given for each user:
- login name,
- tty name,
- the host from which the user logged in. A dash (-) is displayed in the case of a local connection.
- login time. If a user has been connected for over 24 hours, the login time is shown as a day and an hour, without the minutes.
- idle time,
- JCPU time. This is the time accumulated by all processes associated with the terminal. Background jobs that have terminated are not taken into account.
- PCPU time. This is the CPU occupation time for the current process.
- current process (in the WHAT column).

This command is useful to tell you how system loading is distributed amongst the different users.

B. Process management

1. The process concept

A process is an active entity. On the other hand, a program is a passive entity as it is an executable file stored on disk.

Linux distinguishes between two types of process:
– real time processes. A real time process is either preemptible or nonpreemptible.
– normal processes.

It is important to make this distinction between processes when choosing a scheduling policy.

2. Spawning processes

Every process is the child of another process. The child process is created using a mechanism known as spawning. When the system starts up, it creates a process called **init** with a PID of 1. This process is the parent of all other processes on the system, either directly or indirectly. When a process is created, the PID of the parent process that created it is stored in its PPID attribute.

The **pstree** command displays the tree of running processes:

```
[73]-system(merlin)~:pstree
init-+-crond
     |-6*[getty]
     |-2*[gv---gs]
     |-httpd---6*[httpd]
     |-inetd---in.telnetd---bash---pstree
     |-kflushd
     |-klogd
     |-kpiod
     |-kswapd
     |-lpd
     |-md_thread
     |-named
     |-nfsd---lockd---rpciod
     |-postmaster
     |-powerd
     |-rpc.mountd
     |-rpc.portmap
     |-sendmail
     |-syslogd
     |-update
     |-xdm-+-X
     |     '-xdm--.xsession-+-fvwm-+-FvwmPager
     |                      |      |-GoodStuff
     |                      |      |-lyx
     |                      |      |-netscape---netscape
     |                      |      |-xclock
     |                      |      |-xload
     |                      |      |-xterm---bash---bash
     |                      '-xterm---bash-+-more
     |                                     '-xisp
     '-xlock
```

3. Process groups

This concept was introduced to make it easier to handle several processes. A process group is created by a process, which becomes the leader of the group. In addition, the PID of this leader process is used to identify the group created. By default, all processes belong to the same group as their parent process, except those that create their own group. The process group concept has allowed job (or background process) control to be implemented on most modern shells. This is done using a shell built-in command called **kill**.

4. Process states

In contrast to an executable binary file, which is an inert object stored on a disk, a process is an active entity. It requires a certain number of resources: central memory, disk memory and access, other processes...

In common with other time sharing systems, Linux can execute several processes simultaneously. Linux distinguishes between processes that are currently executing and processes that are not executing. Throughout its existence, a process passes through a number of states. Some of these states are obligatory for all processes, others are not. Thus, a process can be:

ready for execution or currently being executed	The process is included in the active processes table (task vector). This means that the process can use the CPU.
Waiting - interruptible	The process is waiting for a resource or an event. It is absent from the active processes table.

kernel version 2.0 to 2.2

Waiting - uninterruptible	Again the process is waiting for a resource or an event and is absent from the active processes table. However, an uninterruptible process cannot be interrupted by a signal (not even by the SIGKILL signal).
Stopped	The process was stopped by an external action. This is generally done by sending a signal.
Zombie	This is a halted process that stays in the system until its parent process receives the return signal. A process can remain in this state forever if the parent process terminates before it. In common with uninterruptible processes, a zombie cannot react to a signal sent to it. However, unlike uninterruptible processes, zombies have terminated their execution and do not consume resources. They remain present in the active process table though. If this table becomes saturated with zombies, the only way to get rid of them is to reboot the system.

5. Scheduling

Scheduling is the mechanism that decides which process will be executed by the CPU. The entity that implements this mechanism is called the scheduler. Processes are chosen for execution according to three criteria:

– process type,
– priority,
– nice index.

When a realtime process becomes ready, it will be executed by the CPU if there is no other realtime process with a higher priority. Two cases are possible:

– The process is of the realtime, nonpreemptible type. In this case it will continue running until one of the following situations occurs:
  – Another process becomes ready, of the same type but with a higher priority. The process that was running is put into a waiting state and the new process is executed.
  – The process needs a resource that is unavailable at present. The process is put into a waiting state.
  – The process suspends its execution itself. In this case it stays in the ready state, but it is placed at the end of the active processes table.
– The process is of the real-time, preemptible type. In this case, the process can be run for a small amount of time called a timeslice. If at the end of this timeslice, there is a realtime process with an equal or higher priority, the new process will be executed instead of the current process. The current process will be reintegrated into the active processes table.

A normal process can be executed only if no realtime process is in the ready state. In this case, the normal process can then use the CPU as long as there are no other processes that are ready with a higher priority.

kernel version 2.0 to 2.2

You can modify the scheduling priority indirectly by modifying the nice index. To do this you can run the command using the **nice** utility. Alternatively, if the process is already running, you can use the **renice** command.

The nice command

By default, the nice index has a value of zero for each user.

> *This is a characteristic of the **login** command, which is part of the shadow software suite.*

On Linux, the value attributed to the nice index varies from -20 to 19. The lower the nice index, the higher the process scheduling priority. Conversely, the higher the nice index, the lower the process scheduling priority. Processes in the latter case will run less quickly than those having a lower nice index.

The **nice** command allows you to execute a process with a nice index other than the default value. Here is the syntax for this command:

```
nice [-n ADJUSTMENT | -ADJUSTMENT] COMMAND
```

If no options are given, the priority of COMMAND will be increased by 10. A different change in this value can be specified in one of the two ways indicated above. The first method, -n ADJUSTMENT is clearer than the second -ADJUSTMENT, which can be confusing. For example, if you specify 5 you will increase the priority by 5 (although you could easily believe you are decreasing the value by 5). To decrease the value by 5 using the second method you must specify -5. Using the first method you would indicate -n 5, which again is clearer.

> *Only the system administrator can decrease the nice index.*

The renice command

This command alters the nice index for one or more processes that are currently running.

It must be noted that a user can apply this command only to his/her own processes. In addition, a user can increase a nice value and cannot decrease it (these two rules do not apply to the system administrator, of course).

Here is the syntax of this command:
```
renice NEW_NICE_INDEX [[-p] PID...] [[-g] PGRP ...]
[[-u] USER...]
```

You can use **renice** to alter nice index(es) for:
- one or more independent processes, by indicating their PIDs,
- all the processes of one or more process groups,
- all the processes belonging to one or more users.

If no option is specified, values supplied will be interpreted as PID's. Groups must be specified following the -g option. User names must be specified following the -u option. The -p option allows you to indicate PIDs explicitly.

You can combine these options in one call to this command. These options can be specified in any order. Here is an example:
```
renice +10 11204 -u user01 user02 -p 5478
```

The above command will assign a nice index of 10 to processes 5478 and 11204 and to all the processes belonging to the users: user01 and user02.

The following command assigns a nice index of 10 to process 21244:

```
system(merlin)~:renice 10 21244
21244: old priority 0, new priority 10
```

The ps command

This command gives a snapshot of active processes. To do this, it uses the active processes table. More or less information can be obtained by specifying different options as follows:

user	The identity of the processes. This can be different from the user owning the process in the case of a SUID process.
pid	The process identifier.
ppid	The identifier of the parent process.
%cpu	Ratio between CPU time and elapsed time.
%mem	Ratio between memory used and memory available.
pri	The scheduling priority index.
ni	The value of the nice index. This can be between -20 (to obtain highest priority) and +19 (to obtain lowest priority).
size	The size of the virtual memory image (=text + data + stack).
rss	Physical memory occupation. This is the resident part of the process in Kbytes.

LINUX Administration

Chapter 7

    wchan   Name of the kernel function that the process is waiting for. By default, this will display the address of the kernel function. However, if the /etc/psdatabase file exists, it will be used to find the association between the address and the name of this kernel function. In this case the name of the kernel function will appear.

    stat   The current status of the process. Up to three characters can be displayed. The first character indicates the state of the process.

The following states can appear:

    R   running.
    S   sleeping (interruptible).
    D   sleeping (uninterruptible, waiting for a resource).
    T   traced or stopped.
    Z   zombie.

A **W** appearing in the second position indicates that the process is completely swapped to disk.

An **N** appearing in the third position indicates that the process is running with a positive nice index. A ">" in the third position indicates that the process is running with a negative nice index (this is the case for the **kswapd** process for example).

    tty   The **tty** of the terminal controlling the process. If the process is not attached to any terminal, a "?" is displayed.

    pagein   The number of page faults. This indicates the number of pages that must be brought from the disk or the cache-buffer.

kernel version 2.0 to 2.2

drs	Size of the data segment resident in memory.
trs	Size of the text segment resident in memory.
swap	Size of the swap used (in Kbytes, or in pages if -p is specified).
shrd	Shared memory.
start	The time the process was started.
time	Accumulated execution time (CPU time).
command	Name of the process, or the command line that created the process. By default this display will be truncated according to the screen size (unless the -w option is specified).

6. The **top** command

Unlike **ps** that shows only a snapshot of the active process table, the **top** command offers an ongoing display of this table in real time. In general, the same information is displayed as for **ps**. The advantage of **top** is that it allows you to monitor processor activity in real time.

7. Sending signals to processes: kill, killall, killall5

Nowadays, on most systems **kill** is a shell built-in command. Notably, this is the case for those shells that have a job control mechanism such as **bash**. One important reason for this is that it can be used to destroy one or more processes when the active process table is full. This is possible because a shell built-in command generates no process. On the other hand, an external **kill** command could not be run in this case as it would be unable to generate the process it would need to execute.

The syntax of this command is relatively simple:

```
kill [-signal] pid ...
```

or

```
kill -l
```

By default, **kill** sends the SIGTERM signal to all the processes indicated by the PID(s) passed as arguments. Another signal may be specified as an option.

The **kill -l** command displays the list of available signals.

```
[29]-system(merlin)~:kill -l
 1) SIGHUP       2) SIGINT      3) SIGQUIT     4) SIGILL
 5) SIGTRAP     6) SIGIOT      7) SIGBUS      8) SIGFPE
 9) SIGKILL    10) SIGUSR1    11) SIGSEGV    12) SIGUSR2
13) SIGPIPE     4) SIGALRM    15) SIGTERM    17) SIGCHLD
18) SIGCONT    19) SIGSTOP    20) SIGTSTP    21) SIGTTIN
22) SIGTTOU    23) SIGURG     24) SIGXCPU    25) SIGXFSZ
26) SIGVTALRM  27) SIGPROF    28) SIGWINCH   29) SIGIO
30) SIGPWR
```

The **killall** command sends a signal to a process that you can identify by its name.

killall5 is the System V version of **killall**. It sends a signal to all processes except those in its own session.

kernel version 2.0 to 2.2

C. Monitoring the memory and the CPU: vmstat

This command displays virtual memory statistics. In addition, it supplies general information on processes and usage of the CPU.

It must be noted that the version of this command currently available on Linux does not have as wide a functionality as that offered by other Unix systems.

Here is the syntax of this command:

```
vmstat [delay [count]]
```

By default, **vmstat** displays its results just once and then exits. However, the `delay` and `count` arguments can be used to repeat the display periodically. The `delay` argument specifies the interval between displays (in seconds) and the `count` argument specifies how many times **vmstat** must display. If `delay` is specified by itself, **vmstat** will run indefinitely.

Here is an example of a **vmstat** display:

```
[75]-system(merlin)~:vmstat 5 5
   procs          memory    swap       io   system    cpu
 r b w  swpd free buff cache si so bi bo  in  cs us sy id
 0 0 0  9220 1208 2052 14080 0  0  3  1 108 113  2  0 98
 0 0 0  9220 1208 2052 14080 0  0  0  0 101 230  1  0 99
 0 0 0  9220 1208 2052 14080 0  0  0  0 101 227  0  1 99
 0 0 0  9220 1208 2052 14080 0  0  0  0 101 230  1  0 99
 0 0 0  9220 1208 2052 14080 0  0  0  0 101 228  1  0 99
```

In all cases, the first data line displayed shows the average values since the system was started. This first line then, does not tell you how the system is running at present. In order to monitor the system, it is advisable to specify several displays using the `delay` and `count` arguments. You can even create a function so that the first data line will not be displayed, as in the following example:

```
[32]-system(merlin)~:vm(){
>vmstat $* | awk 'NR!=3'
>}
[33]-system(merlin)~:vm 5 5
 procs        memory      swap        io     system      cpu
 rbw  swpd  free buff cache si so  bi bo  in  cs us sy id
 000  9220  1232 1912 14104 0  0   24 0  103 229 0  1  99
 000  9220  1232 1912 14104 0  0   0  0  101 230 0  1  99
 000  9220  1228 1916 14104 0  0   0  0  102 229 0  1  99
 000  9220  1228 1916 14104 0  0   0  0  101 229 0  1  99
```

The columns are grouped together under six headings:

procs   These colums show statistics on active processes:

         r   The number of processes waiting to be executed.

         b   The number of processes in uninterruptible waiting (sleep) state. These processes are generally awaiting inputs/outputs.

         w   The number of executable processes that are currently swapped-out. This field should never be different from zero (0).

memory   These columns show statistics on memory usage:

         swpd   Virtual memory used (in Kbytes).

         free   virtual memory available (in Kbytes).

         buff   Virtual memory used as buffers (in Kbytes).

swap			These columns show statistics on virtual memory activity:
	si		Memory swapped-in from disk (in Kbytes).
	so		Memory swapped-out to disk (in Kbytes).
io			These columns show statistics on input/output activity (of all block devices together):
	bi		Number of blocks read per second from a block device.
	bo		Number of blocks written per second to a block device.
system			These columns show statistics on general system activity:
	in		Number of interruptions per second.
	cs		Number of context changes per second.
cpu			These columns show statistics on CPU usage:
	us		User time as a percentage of total CPU time.
	sy		System time as a percentage of total CPU time.
	id		idle time as a percentage of total CPU time

The advantage of **vmstat** over the **procinfo** command is that the former displays information only on crucial system items that could cause a bottleneck (i.e. memory, input/output and the CPU).

It must be remembered that high values displayed at any given time may not be representative of the general running of the system. They must be compared with other snapshots taken at other times. It might also be interesting to take and save such snapshots for future reference and analysis. The **cron** utility can be used for this purpose.

D. Disk space monitoring

1. The `df` command

This command displays a summary of disk space usage for a file system whose name is passed as an argument. By default, the command displays disk space usage for the complete set of file systems:

```
[48]-system(merlin)~:df
Filesystem  1024-blocks  Used  Available  Capacity  Mounted on
/dev/hdc2   1387050   1188004   127352    90%    /
/dev/hdc3     87241     14636    68095    18%    /var
/dev/hdc4     28299      2730    24108    10%    /tmp
/dev/sda1    515433    471138    17672    96%    /home
/dev/hdd     260150    260150        0   100%    /cdrom
```

The following information is displayed by default for each file system:

- the special file used,
- the total number of blocks,
- the number of occupied blocks,
- the number of blocks available,
- the percentage of space occupied,
- the mount point.

The block size is 1024 bytes by default. This is the standard size for the `df` command on BSD type systems. You can change this default value to 512 bytes by setting the POSIXLY_CORRECT variable to "y".

```
[49]-system(merlin)~:export POSIXLY_CORRECT=y
[50]-system(merlin)~:df
Filesystem  512-blocks   Used  Available  Capacity  Mounted on
/dev/hdc2   2774100   2376008   254704    90%    /
/dev/hdc3    174482     29272   136190    18%    /var
/dev/hdc4     56598      5460    48216    10%    /tmp
/dev/sda1   1030866    942276    35344    96%    /home
/dev/hdd     520300    520300        0   100%    /cdrom
```

Here is a selection of the options most commonly used with this command:

- `-a` To display information on file systems that occupy no blocks. By default, no information is displayed for such file systems. These are generally pseudo file systems such as the /proc directory.
- `-i` To display file system occupation statistics in terms of numbers of inodes rather than numbers of blocks.
- `-k` To specify a block size of 1024 bytes. This option is useful when the POSIXLY_CORRECT variable has been set to "y" (default block size of 512 bytes).
- `-T` To display the type of each file system.
- `-t fstype` To display information only for *fstype* file systems. You can specify `-t` several times to specify several types of file system.
- `-x fstype` Not to display information for *fstype* file systems (the opposite of `-t`).

Chapter 7

```
[53]-system(merlin)~:df -i
Filesystem    Inodes   IUsed   IFree   %IUsed  Mounted on
/dev/hdc2     359800   58803   300997  6%      /
/dev/hdc3     22616      998   21618   4%      /var
/dev/hdc4      7328       41    7287   1%      /tmp
/dev/sda1     133120   23419   109701  18%     /home
/dev/hdd           0       0        0  0%      /cdrom
/dev/fd0           0       0        0  0%      /mnt
[54]-system(merlin)~:df -T
Filesystem Type 512-blocks Used Available Capacity Mounted on
/dev/hdc2  ext2    2774100 2376008 254704      90%    /
/dev/hdc3  ext2     174482   29272 136190      18%    /var
/dev/hdc4  ext2      56598    5460  48216      10%    /tmp
/dev/sda1  ext2    1030866  942276  35344      96%    /home
/dev/hdd   iso9660  520300  520300      0     100%    /cdrom
/dev/fd0   vfat       2847     117   2730       4%    /mnt
[55]-system(merlin)~:df -xvfat
Filesystem 512-blocks  Used Available Capacity Mounted on
/dev/hdc2    2774100 2376008   254704     90%    /
/dev/hdc3     174482   29272   136190     18%    /var
/dev/hdc4      56598    5460    48216     10%    /tmp
/dev/sda1    1030866  942276    35344     96%    /home
/dev/hdd      520300  520300        0    100%    /cdrom
[56]-system(merlin)~:df -xvfat -T
Filesystem Type 512-blocks Used Available Capacity Mounted on
/dev/hdc2  ext2    2774100 2376008 254704      90%    /
/dev/hdc3  ext2     174482   29272 136190      18%    /var
/dev/hdc4  ext2      56598    5460  48216      10%    /tmp
/dev/sda1  ext2    1030866  942276  35344      96%    /home
/dev/hdd   iso9660  520300  520300      0     100%    /cdrom
```

Resource management

kernel version 2.0 to 2.2

2. The du command

Whereas the **df** command reports on the general usage of file systems, the **du** command provides details of this usage.

du provides space usage information for the file or directory passed as an argument. This information is given recursively in the case of a directory. If no argument is given, the information is displayed for the current directory. The information is given in numbers of blocks of 1024 bytes by default. As with **df**, You can change this default value to 512 bytes by setting the POSIXLY_CORRECT variable to "y".

```
[62]-system(merlin)~:du cours/c/exo
1          cours/c/exo/signal
14         cours/c/exo/strings
2          cours/c/exo/arg
4          cours/c/exo/bit
18         cours/c/exo/list
49         cours/c/exo/files
13         cours/c/exo/errors
27         cours/c/exo/misc
339        cours/c/exo/posix
476        cours/c/exo
[63]-system(merlin)~:export POSIXLY_CORRECT=y
[64]-system(merlin)~:du cours/c/exo
2          cours/c/exo/signal
28         cours/c/exo/strings
4          cours/c/exo/arg
8          cours/c/exo/bit
36         cours/c/exo/list
98         cours/c/exo/files
26         cours/c/exo/errors
54         cours/c/exo/misc
678        cours/c/exo/posix
952        cours/c/exo
```

Chapter 7

The following options allow you to adapt the functioning of the **du** command:

- `-a` To display information on all files and not only on directories.
- `-b` To display file system usage in bytes.

```
[90]-system(merlin)~:du -b cours/c/exo
1024     cours/c/exo/signal
11042    cours/c/exo/strings
1171     cours/c/exo/arg
2638     cours/c/exo/bit
14208    cours/c/exo/list
41907    cours/c/exo/files
10422    cours/c/exo/errors
21053    cours/c/exo/misc
334280   cours/c/exo/posix
444759   cours/c/exo
```

- `-c` To display a grand total of individual occupation totals.

```
[91]-system(merlin)~:du /bin /sbin
9420     /bin
5282     /sbin
[92]-system(merlin)~:du -c /bin /sbin
9420     /bin
5282     /sbin
14702    total
```

- `-k` To specify a block size of 1024 bytes. This option is useful when the POSIXLY_CORRECT variable has been set to "y" (default block size of 512 bytes).

```
[93]-system(merlin)~:du -k cours/c/exo
1        cours/c/exo/signal
14       cours/c/exo/strings
2        cours/c/exo/arg
4        cours/c/exo/bit
18       cours/c/exo/list
49       cours/c/exo/files
13       cours/c/exo/errors
27       cours/c/exo/misc
339      cours/c/exo/posix
476      cours/c/exo
```

Resource management

kernel version 2.0 to 2.2

-l To consider physical links as files in their own right and to take their size into account when determining the disk occupation of the parent directory.

-s To display only the total occupation for each argument.

-x To skip directories on file systems other than that concerned by the directory passed as an argument.

-D To specify that, when a symbolic link is passed as an argument, the target file must be taken into account rather than the link itself.

```
[110]-system(merlin)~:file /usr/tmp
/usr/tmp: symbolic link to /var/tmp
[111]-system(merlin)~:du /usr/tmp
0        /usr/tmp
[112]-system(merlin)~:du -D /usr/tmp
2        /usr/tmp/.pop
32       /usr/tmp
```

-L To specify that, when the **du** command finds a symbolic link in a directory, the target file must be taken into account rather than the link itself.

-S To exclude subdirectories in the size calculations.

```
[113]-system(merlin)~: du /tmp
2        /tmp/.X11-unix
5382     /tmp/lyx_tmp178aaa/lyx_bufrtmp178aaa
5390     /tmp/lyx_tmp178aaa
12       /tmp/wpc-merlin
5456     /tmp
[114]-system(merlin)~:du -s /tmp
5456     /tmp
[115]-system(merlin)~:du -sS /tmp
52       /tmp
```

E. Monitoring the swap: **swapon**, **free**

In order to maintain optimal performance levels, it is important to monitor usage of the swap area. The more often this area is used, the more often the disk will be accessed. Frequent disk accessing causes the general performance of the system to deteriorate.

Since kernel version 2.1.25, the **swapon** command offers the -s option. This option lists swap usage statistics by device:

```
[116]-system(merlin)~:swapon -s
Filename        Type          Size      Used      Priority
/dev/hdc1       partition     33228     12892     -1
```

In the above example, the swap area is not used very often. This indicates that the system has sufficient physical memory.

The **free** utility may also be used to display amounts of free and used memory in the system.

↓personal notes↓

Chapter 8

Management of the printing system

A.	The line printer daemon: **lpd**	**161**
B.	Printer service configuration: */etc/printcap*	**161**
C.	Control files	**165**
D.	Printing command: **lpr**	**168**
E.	Spool queue management: **lpq, lprm**	**169**
	1. Listing print jobs: **lpq**	**169**
	2. Removing print jobs: **lprm**	**170**
F.	Administrating the printing system: **lpc**	**170**
G.	Remote printing	**173**
	1. On the local site	**173**
	2. On the remote site	**174**

kernel version 2.0 to 2.2

A printing system is generally composed of the following items:

- Commands to start printing.
- Spool queues to store print jobs and allow them to be processed sequentially. In its simplest form, a spool queue is a serie of jobs waiting to use a specific peripheral device.
- Spool directories that contain the jobs waiting to be processed. On BSD systems, a copy of the file to be printed is included in these directories. On the other hand, AIX and System V store only a small job file in these directories. The file to be printed will be read from its original directory as and when it is required for printing.
- Server processes that are in charge of taking queued jobs and processing them on the device concerned.
- Administration commands.

There are two types of printing subsystems on Unix systems: the BSD type and the System V type. The configuration of a printing system varies according to this system type as the commands and the files are not the same in both cases.

Linux printing subsystems have always conformed to the BSD model. This model is based on the socket concept.

A. The line printer daemon: lpd

The entire Linux printing service is run by this daemon. Consequently, **lpd** is started upon system boot. This is done automatically using an initialisation script after the system goes into multi-user mode. In the case of a Slackware distribution, the */etc/rc.d/rc.M* script is used. For RedHat distributions, this function is provided by the */etc/rc.d/init.d/lpd* script. This script is pointed to by the S65lpd links in the */etc/rc.d/rc[2345].d* directory.

There can be only one **lpd** daemon running on a system. To ensure this, **lpd** indicates its presence by creating the */var/spool/lpd/lpd.lock* file.

As soon as it is started, **lpd** starts listening to the */dev/printer* socket in order to respond to local printing requests (jobs). When **lpd** receives a request, it creates a child process to deal with it and then continues listening for the next request.

lpd also processes print requests coming from the network. It does this by listening on the 515 port, defined under the name of **printer** in the */etc/services* file. For a request to be acceptable, the site sending the request must be included either in the */etc/hosts.equiv* or the */etc/hosts.lpd* file.

B. Printer service configuration: /etc/printcap

This file defines the printing characteristics of the various system printers. It includes the following parameters:
- the logical name of the printer,
- the printer's special interface file,
- the spool access path,

- various other parameters (covered in the following pages).

This file is supplied with the system and generally defines a large number of configurations. Here is an extract from this file:

```
lp|defautlt printer:\
:lp=/dev/lp1:\
:sd=/usr/spool/lp1:\
:af=/var/account/lp-acct:\
:lf=/var/log/lpd-err:\
:rs:\
:mx#0:\
:sh
#
# Printer Epson Stylus Color 600 - 20/02/1998
# Filter to process postscript files
#
esps|espon for postscript files:\
:lp=/dev/lp1:\
:sd=/usr/spool/esps:\
:af=/var/account/esps-acct:\
:if=/usr/spool/esps/filter.ps:\
:rs:\:mx#0:\
:sh
```

The */etc/printcap* file is organised by lines. Each line contains the print characteristics of a particular printer and is composed of a number of fields separated by colons (:). However, as these fields can be numerous, a definition can extend over several physical lines. In this case the continuation character ("\") must appear to terminate each line that is to be continued on the following line.

The first field of a printer definition contains its name. This begins with the printer's short name, a maximum of four characters long. It can be followed by one or two long names separated from the short name and from each other by the "|" character.

Supplementary fields may be added after this first field. The presence of a field allows you to modify its default value (cf. the table below).

Each field has a two-character name. There are three types of field:

− string fields. These fields have the following syntax:
```
name=character_string
```

− numerical fields. These fields have the following syntax:
```
name#value
```

− boolean fields. These fields can have a value of true or false. Their presence indicates the value (generally true) that is the opposite of their default value (generally false). These fields are defined simply by their names:
```
name
```

The following table describes the main fields that can be used in this file:

Name	Type	Default value	Description
hl	boolean	false	print a separation page (burst header page) after each job (provided that **sh** is not specified).
if	string	NULL	name of the text filter used for accounting.
lf	string	/dev/console	name of the error logging file.
lp	string	/dev/lp	name of the special file on which the jobs are output.
mx	numerical	1000	maximum file size (in units of BUFSIZ blocks). A value of zero (0) indicates unlimited size.
pl	numerical	66	(page length) number of lines per page.

kernel version 2.0 to 2.2

Name	Type	Default value	Description
pw	numerical	132	(page width) number of characters per line.
rg	string	NULL	(restricted group) usage of the printer is restricted to members of the specified group.
rm	string	NULL	name of the machine hosting the remote printer.
rp	string	lp	name of the remote printer.
rs	boolean	false	remote printing is restricted to users with local accounts.
sc	boolean	false	multiple copies are not authorised.
sd	string	/var/spool/lpd	name of the spool directory.
sh	boolean	false	no printing of a separation page (burst header page) after each job.

For further details, consult the **printcap** manual page (5).

C. Control files

These files allow print system commands to communicate with each other.

The first of these files is */var/spool/lpd/lpd.lock*. As mentioned at the beginning of this chapter, this file prevents more than one parent **lpd** daemon from running on the system. This is the only general control file. All the other files are dedicated to a spool queue and provide information on this spool queue. These include the following three files:

lock

The *lock* file contains at least one line. This line shows the PID of the last **lpd** process that handled the spool queue concerned. The second line contains the name of the job configuration file of the current print job. Alternatively, it can contain the name of the last print job if this job was stopped.

lock is the default name for this file. You can choose another name using the **lo** field in */etc/printcap*.

In the following example, the printing was suspended. The *lock* file contains two lines. The first line shows the PID of the **lpd** process created to deal with the print request. The second line contains the name of the job configuration file for this print request.

```
# cat lock
1423
cfA318Aa01416
# ps aux|grep lpd
root  89   0.0 0.6 788 312 ? S 11:20 0:00 /usr/sbin/lpd
root  1423 0.0 0.8 804 380 ? S 19:52 0:00 /usr/sbin/
lpd
```

kernel version 2.0 to 2.2

The second part of this example shows two **lpd** processes. The process with a PID of 89 is the parent process. This process is started when the system boots. It creates a new child process to deal with each print request. In this case, the child process created has a PID of 1423.

This file is locked to ensure that the request is dealt with by only one **lpd** daemon. This locking mechanism also ensures that requests for the printer concerned are handled sequentially.

The **lpq** and **lpr** commands interpret the *lock* file access permissions to determine the status of the spool queue and the printer. This is done as follows:
- if the owner has execution permission, then printing is disabled,
- if the group has execution permission, then the spool queue is closed,
- the above situations can be combined.

status

The *status* file provides information on the status of the printer. It is consulted by the **lpq** and **lpr** commands.

Here is an example of this file:

```
# cat status
printing disabled
```

In this example, the *status* file indicates that printing has been suspended on the printer concerned. Nevertheless, print requests will still be accepted and will be placed in the spool queue.

status is the default name for this file. You can choose another name using the **st** field in */etc/printcap*.

.seq

The *.seq* file contains the number of the next print job. The **lpr** command uses this file to number job files. Requests coming from a distant site are numbered on the distant site sending the request.

```
# ls -l
total 5
-rw-rw----  1 bin     lp      76 Nov  8 19:52 cfA318Aa01416
-rw-rw----  1 system  lp     678 Nov  8 19:52 dfA318Aa01416
-rwxr-xr-x  1 root    root    76 May  9  1998 filter.ps* -
rwxr--r--   1 root    root    19 Nov  8 19:52 lock*
-rw-rw-r--  1 root    root    18 Nov  8 19:53 status
# cat .seq
319
```

In addition, two further files are created for each request:

— The first of these files is simply a copy of the file to be printed. Its name is composed of the following elements:
  — a two letter prefix,
  — a letter from A to Z,
  — a sequential number taken from the *.seq* file,
  — a suffix identifying the site that sent the request,
  — the prefix is generally **df**. This gives 26 possible files, from dfA to dfZ. If the print request was made specifying the -s option, then this file is a link to the file to be printed.
— The second file contains a certain number of parameters concerning the printing itself.

D. Printing command: **lpr**

This command requests the printing of the file. The name of the file to be printed can be supplied as an argument. Alternatively, **lpr** can work with its standard input. This allows you to use this command in a pipeline. For example, you can print the contents of the current directory as follows:

```
$ ls | lpr
$
```

All this command does, is to add the print request to the spool queue of the printer by default. Alternatively, the user can choose to send the print request to another printer. If this printer is required only occasionally, the user can specify it using the `-P printer_name` option of the **lpr** command. Alternatively, if this printer is required frequently, it is preferable to specify the printer name in the PRINTER environment variable. This printer then becomes the user's printer by default.

This command offers a number of options. Here is a list of those most frequently used:

- `-P` designates a specific printer (cf. above). If this option is not specified, the default printer will be used, unless another printer has been specified in your PRINTER environment variable.
- `-m` requests that you are notified when the printing is completed. This option is useful when you request your job to be printed later or if the spool queue is very long.
- `-r` deletes the file after it has been printed (this option cannot be combined with `-s`).

`-s` requests **lpr** to use the specified file directly, instead of making a copy. This option is useful when the file is large. However, if you specify this option, it is better not to modify the file's contents before the printing has finished.

`-#num` requests that `num` copies are printed.

E. Spool queue management: lpq, lprm

The **lpq** commands allow the user to list the documents that have been submitted to spool queues. If required, the **lprm** command allows the user to delete items from spool queues.

1. Listing print jobs: lpq

When called without option or argument, this command lists the spool queue, either for the **lp** printer, or for the printer specified in $PRINTER. If you want to view a specific spool queue, you can indicate the queue concerned using the `-p` option.

```
$ lpq
Rank    Owner      Job    Files          Total Size
1st     system     503    bug.c          678 bytes
2nd     root       504    linux_admin    10549 bytes
```

lpq displays the following information:
— current rank in the spool queue
— the user who requested the print
— the job number
— the name of the file to be printed
— the size of the file to be printed

kernel version 2.0 to 2.2

The job number is necessary if you want to delete the job from the spool queue. To do this you can use the **lprm** command.

2. Removing print jobs: **lprm**

This is the only command that allows a user to remove a job from a spool queue. The job to be removed is indicated by the job number that is supplied as an argument to this command. By default, the job is removed from the **lp** spool queue or from that specified in $PRINTER. As with **lpr** and **lpq**, you can specify another spool queue using the -P option.

A user can remove only those jobs that he/she submitted. The user can remove all the requests that he/she submitted by specifying the - option.

Only the system administrator is allowed to remove jobs submitted by other users. This is done by indicating the user name to the **lprm** command.

F. Administrating the printing system: **lpc**

Administrating BSD printing systems can involve the following tasks:

- Activating or deactivating a printer. This does not affect the spool queue associated. You must distinguish clearly between printers and physical printing devices. Two printers can share the same physical printing device.
- Activating or deactivating a spool queue. If you deactivate a spool queue, all future print requests to the queue will be refused. The jobs already present in the queue will be processed if the associated printer is active.

- Modifying the rank of jobs in a spool queue.
- Displaying the status of the various printers, spool queues and associated processes.

All administration tasks for a BSD printing system are carried out using the **lpc** command. This command has two functioning modes according to whether it is called with or without arguments.

When called without arguments, **lpc** goes into interactive mode. It displays the `lpc>` prompt and awaits a command. When you have finished entering commands, you must close the **lpc** command explicitly. Alternatively, you can call **lpc**, specifying an action as an argument. In this case, **lpc** will execute your requested action and then terminate. This mode is sufficient in many situations.

Here are the actions that the **lpc** command can execute:

? [cmd], help[cmd]	Provides online help, either general, or concerning the command supplied as an argument.
abort {all|printer}	Stops the current print job immediately and deactivates printing for the printer(s) indicated as an argument.
stop {all|printer}	Completes the current print job and deactivates printing for the printer(s) indicated as an argument.
start {all|printer}	Activates the printer(s) indicated as an argument. The spool queues are unchanged.
restart {all|printer}	Has the same effect as **start** except that existing **lpd** processes are stopped and new ones are started.
disable {all|printer}	Deactivates the spool queue(s) indicated as an argument. This prevents new jobs from being put into the queue.
enable {all|printer}	Activates the spool queue(s) indicated as an argument. This allows new jobs to be put into the queue.

kernel version 2.0 to 2.2

down {all|printer} message	Deactivates the spool queue(s) and printer(s) and puts the message into the printer(s) status file. The contents of this file can be displayed using the **lpq** command.
up {all|printer}	Activates the spool queue(s) and printer(s) indicated.
topq printer [jobnum] [user]	Puts the indicated jobs to the top of the indicated spool queue. If a user name is given, all the user's requests will be put to the top of the indicated spool queue.
status {all|printer}	Displays the status of the spool queue(s) and **lpd** daemons for the printer(s) indicated.
clean {all|printer}	Cleans the spool queue(s) indicated, by removing all temporary, data and control files for jobs that cannot be printed.
exit, quit	Close the interactive **lpc** session.

```
[merlin]# lpc down esps printer maintenance
esps: printer and queuing disabled
[merlin]# lpq -Pesps
Warning: esps is down: printer maintenance
Warning: esps queue is turned off, no entries
[merlin]#
```

G. Remote printing

You can request that a document is printed on a remote printer (a remote printer is one that is not connected directly to your local machine). In this case, the **lpd** daemon of the local machine will transmit the request to the **lpd** daemon of the remote machine where the document is to be printed.

1. On the local site

A remote printer is declared by making a fresh entry in the */etc/printcap* file, in the same way as a local printer would be declared.

The following example show two entries in this file that declare remote printers:

```
lp:\
lp=:\
sd=/var/spool/lpd:\
rm=merlin.dorset.fr:\
rp=lp:mx#0:\
sh:
esps|Postscript printer:\
:lp=/dev/null:\
:sd=/var/spool/esps:\
:rp=esps:\
:rm=merlin.dorset.fr:\
:mx#0:
```

The following points must be noted:
- The **lp** field is empty. As the printer is not physically connected to the local machine, you do not need to provide information for this field.
- The **rm** field indicates the remote machine to which the printer is connected.
- The **rp** field indicates the name of the remote printer on the remote machine.

- The **sd** field creates a spool directory for the printer. A spool directory is required, even though the printer is not connected locally.
- No further details are required. The characteristics of the printer are indicated in the remote printer configuration file.

2. On the remote site

To enable a local printer to be used by remote sites, the names of the remote sites must be included either in the /etc/hosts.lpd or in the /etc/hosts.equiv file.

If it exists, the /etc/hosts.lpd file is read first. Only those sites appearing in this file will be allowed to use the local printer.

If /etc/hosts.lpd does not exist, the /etc/hosts.equiv file will be consulted.

To improve the security of the printer site, you can stipulate that only those users that have an account on the printer site will be allowed to use specified printers. To do this, include the `rs` field in the required entries of the /etc/printcap file on the printer site.

Chapter 9

Terminal management

A.	Introduction	176
B.	The getty daemon	177
	1. Running **getty**	178
	2. The */etc/gettydefs* file	179
C.	Defining terminals	181
	1. termcap databases	182
	2. terminfo databases	183
	3. termcap versus terminfo	183
	4. The **toe** command	184
	5. The **infocmp** command	186
	6. The **tic** command	188

kernel version 2.0 to 2.2

A. Introduction

In common with other Unix systems, Linux handles different types of terminal:
– virtual consoles
– serial terminals
– pseudo terminals
– X terminals...

It may be necessary to have a backup terminal ready for use in the event of the system terminal locking up. In this case, you can use the backup terminal to open a session and resolve the problem. However, it may not even be possible to log in to the system. In this case, all you can do is reset the system by interrupting its power supply (in spite of the risk of corrupting the file system).

This chapter describes how to connect a serial terminal to the system. The vt100 type was chosen as an example.

Linux has several terminal management daemons. These include **agetty**, **getty_ps** and **mgetty**. In this chapter, we will cover the **getty_ps** daemon. This daemon is similar to the classical **getty** daemon of Unix System V.

B. The getty daemon

The **getty** process listens to terminals and runs the following login procedure:

- display the prelogin message contained in */etc/issue*.
- display the login prompt indicated in */etc/gettydefs/* (this is generally **login**:).
- wait for a character string confirmed by a newline or carriage-return character.
- start the login process, which terminates the procedure.
- display the contents of the */etc/notd* file (if the *$HOME/.hushlogin* file is absent).
- start the login shell.

In the case of repeated failure or on expiry of a timeout, the login process terminates and **init** starts a fresh **getty** process for this terminal (provided that this is requested by the presence of the **respawn** keyword in */etc/inittab*).

getty is a direct child process of the **init** process. Execution of the **getty** process is defined by a set of entries in the */etc/inittab* file. The functionalities of the **getty** process are determined by parameters contained in the */etc/gettydefs* file.

Here is an example extract from the /etc/inittab file concerning the **getty** command:

```
#
# Virtual consoles
#
c1:1235:respawn:/sbin/getty tty1 VC linux
c2:1235:respawn:/sbin/getty tty2 VC linux
c3:12345:respawn:/sbin/getty tty3 VC linux
c4:12345:respawn:/sbin/getty tty4 VC linux
c5:12345:respawn:/sbin/getty tty5 VC linux
c6:12345:respawn:/sbin/getty tty6 VC linux
c7:12345:respawn:/sbin/getty tty7 VC linux
c8:12345:respawn:/sbin/getty tty8 VC linux
#
# serial lines
#
s1:2345:respawn:/sbin/getty ttyS1 DT9600 vt100
s2:2345:respawn:/sbin/getty ttyS2 DT9600 vt100
s3:2345:respawn:/sbin/getty ttyS3 DT9600 vt100
s4:2345:respawn:/sbin/getty ttyS4 DT9600 vt100
```

1. Running getty

There are two ways of running the **getty** command:

- You can run it manually so as to check the syntax of the **getty** configuration file.
- You can run it automatically, using the /etc/inittab file, to manage the connection lines.

Manual execution

Checking the syntax of the **getty** daemon's configuration file is essential. Any error in this file can prevent all logins to the system. You can be reasonably confident that a configuration file will be correct in its original state as delivered with the daemon. However, you must check this file if you modify it with your own configurations.

Automatic execution

The */etc/inittab* file is used for this purpose. This file indicates to the **init** process, the actions that must be carried out. These actions generally concern system startup.

This file specifies that **getty** must be run using the following syntax:

```
/sbin/getty    line    label
```

>   `line` is the name of the special file managing the interface with the physical terminal. This special file must be in the */dev* directory.
>
>   `label` is an entry in the */etc/gettydefs* file that defines the principal login characteristics.

Further details on the various **getty** options can be found in the **getty** manual page. However, in most cases, **getty** is called as described above.

The system administrator can deactivate a terminal as follows:

— replace the *respawn* keyword by the *off* keyword on the line concerned in the */etc/inittab* file,
— run the **telinit** command to request **init** to read this configuration file.

2. The */etc/gettydefs* file

This file contains various login parameters and the login prompt. The characteristics contained in this file provide for several types of login.

Each entry in this file contains five fields separated by hash (#) characters:

```
label#initialflags#finalflags#loginprompt#nextlabel
```

Each entry must be followed by a blank line. A line that begins with a hash (#) is ignored and may be used for comments.

Here is a description of these fields:

- **label**: This field identifies the entry. This field is used by **getty** to identify the entry indicated by its second argument. This field often contains the terminal speed (example: 9600). However, this need not be the case.
- **initialflags**: This field contains the initial login settings that will be supplied to **getty** by the **ioctl()** function. The **termios** manual page details the list of flags you can use in this field.
- **finalflags**: This field contains the login settings that will be applied just before the login process. You can use the same values for **finalflags** as for **initialflags**.
- **loginprompt**: This is the character string that will be displayed as the login prompt. This field generally contains the string login:. The display of this field must not be confused with that of the pre-login message contained in the /etc/issue file (cf. the beginning of this section).
- **nextlabel**: This field contains the **label** of another entry in the table. **getty** must use this next entry if the user input cannot be read or if the user types a **<break>**. Entries are linked together in this way so that alternative settings may be tried out, such as different speeds.

Here is an example extract from the /etc/gettydefs file:

```
# Virtual Console entry
VC# B9600 SANE CLOCAL # B9600 SANE -ISTRIP CLOCAL #
@S login: #VC

# 38400 fixed baud Dumb Terminal entry
DT38400# B38400 CS8 CLOCAL CRTSCTS # B38400 SANE
-ISTRIP CLOCAL CRTSCTS #@S logi
n: #DT38400

# 19200 fixed baud Dumb Terminal entry
DT19200# B19200 CS8 CLOCAL # B19200 SANE -ISTRIP
 CLOCAL #@S login: #DT19200

# 9600 baud Dumb Terminal entry
DT9600# B9600 CS8 CLOCAL # B9600 SANE -ISTRIP
CLOCAL #@S login: #DT9600
DT1200# B1200 CS8 CLOCAL # B1200 SANE -ISTRIP
CLOCAL #@S login: #DT1200

# 38400 fixed-baud modem entry
F38400# B38400 CS8 # B38400 SANE -ISTRIP HUPCL
#@S login: #F38400
```

C. Defining terminals

Each terminal has specific physical characteristics that must be available for consultation by any process that wishes to access the terminal. For this purpose, these characteristics are stored in a database.

On Unix systems, two types of database are used to manage terminals:

— BSD type systems use the /etc/termcap file.
— System V type systems use a file hierarchy starting at /usr/share/terminfo.

The database that is used in any given instance depends on the individual program concerned. Consequently, in common with AIX and other Unix systems, Linux uses both types of database.

1. termcap databases

The termcap database is contained in the single file: /etc/termcap. This file defines all the terminals that the system is capable of managing.

Each definition is contained on one logical line. This logical line can extend over several physical lines. Each physical line that is continued onto the next physical line is terminated by a backslash (\) character. Here is an example extract from the /etc/termcap file:

```
# cat /etc/termcap
...
# Generic VT entry.
vg|vt-generic|Generic VT entries:\
        :bs:mi:ms:pt:xn:xo:it#8:\
        :RA=\E[?71:SA=\E?7h:\
        :bl=^G:cr=^M:ta=^I:\
        :cm=\E[%i%d;%dH:\
        :le=^H:up=\E[A:do=\E[B:nd=\E[C:\
        :LE=\E[%dD:RI=\E[%dC:UP=\E[%dA:DO=\E[%dB:\
        :ho=\E[H:cl=\E[H\E[2J:ce=\E[K:cb=\E[1K:cd=\
        E[J:sf=\ED:sr=\EM:\
        :ct=\E[3g:st=\EH:\
        :cs=\E[%i%d;%dr:sc=\E7:rc=\E8:\
        :ei=\E[4l:ic=\E[@:IC=\E[%d@:al=\E[L:AL=\
        E[%dL:\
        :dc=\E[P:DC=\E[%dP:dl=\E[M:DL=\E[%dM:\
        :so=\E[7m:se=\E[m:us=\E[4m:ue=\E[m:\
        :mb=\E[5m:mh=\E[2m:md=\E[1m:mr=\E[7m:me=\
        E[m:\
        :sc=\E7:rc=\E8:kb=\177:\
        :ku=\E[A:kd=\E[B:kr=\E[C:kl=\E[D:...
```

The entry selected in this file depends on the **TERM** environment variable, which contains a terminal name.

Another environment variable that is used is called **TERMCAP**. This variable can contain the name of an alternative configuration file. It can also contain the definition of the terminal used, directly. This technique avoids reading the /etc/termcap file, each time a process needs to find out the configuration of the current terminal. This can save a lot of time, especially if the definition concerned is situated towards the end of the file.

However, if the **TERMCAP** variable is not set, the /etc/termcap file will be used by default.

2. terminfo databases

The terminfo database is made up of a set of files. Each file represents a terminal. It is named after the terminal and it contains a definition of the terminal. These files are organised into a hierarchy. Each of these files is contained in a directory with a one-character name. The directory name is the same as the first character of the file name. This set of directories is contained in the /usr/share/terminfo directory.

Each file is the result of a compilation from a source file by the **tic** utility (**t**erminfo **c**ompiler). Consequently, you cannot read these database files unless you decompile them using the **infocmp** command. Information on a specific terminal can be accessed rapidly by a process. This is because of the organisation of these files and the fact that they are compiled objects.

3. termcap versus terminfo

In contrast to the terminfo database, the sequential organisation of the /etc/termcap file means that definitions towards the end of the file take longer to retrieve. Consequently, it is advisable to place at the beginning of this file the definition of those terminals that are used the most.

Similarly, those terminals that are not used at all should be either deleted or placed at the end of the file. Eventually, the terminfo database will completely replace the /etc/termcap file. However, this file must be kept on the system as some programs still use it.

4. The toe command

The **toe** command allows you to obtain information from the terminfo database. Here is the syntax of this command:

```
toe [options] [file]
```

When called without options or arguments, **toe** displays the list of all the terminals contained in this database. This list is made from the database in its default location (/usr/share/terminfo). The primary name of each terminal is given along with a brief definition (cf. the example below).

The -h option allows you to check the location by default:

```
[3]-system(merlin)~:toe|grep vt100|head
vt100           dec vt100 (w/advanced video)
vt100           dec vt100 (w/advanced video)
vt220           DEC VT220 in vt100 emulation mode
v5410           5410 in terms of a vt100
versaterm       versaterm vt100 emulator
                for the macintosh
vt100nam        vt100 no automargins
vt100-w         dec vt100 132 cols (w/advanced video)
vt100-w-nam     dec vt100 132 cols (w/advanced video
                no automargin)
vt100-nav       vt100 without advanced video option
vt100-nav-w     dec vt100 132 cols 14 lines
                (no advanced video option)
[4]-system(merlin)~:toe -h | head
#
#/home/system/.terminfo:
#
vt100           dec vt100 (w/advanced video)
#
#/usr/lib/terminfo:
#
lpr             line printer
lisa            apple lisa console display
                (black on white)
ln03            dec ln03 laser printer
```

The **toe** utility also offers the following options:

- -u Displays the dependencies of the definition file passed as an argument. These dependencies are the terminals on which the definitions depend. It must be noted that the file passed as an argument, must have been decompiled previously by **infocmp**.
- -U Displays the reverse dependencies of the definition file passed as an argument. These reverse dependencies are the terminals that depend on the definitions. Again, the file passed as an argument must have been decompiled previously by **infocmp**.

-v[n]   Displays (verbose) information on progress made by **toe**. The n argument is an integer from 1 to 10. It specifies the amount of information to be displayed. The higher this number the more information is output.

5. The infocmp command

infocmp allows you to view the contents of a file from the terminfo database. This command has the following syntax:

infocmp   [options]   [terminal_name]

infocmp is generally used to provide a starting point to produce a description for a terminal that is not already in the database. Consequently, the results of this command are usually redirected to a file so that they can be modified to correspond to the new terminal.

The example below shows **infocmp** being used to obtain the characteristics of the vt100 terminal:

```
5]-system(merlin)~:infocmp vt100
#       Reconstructed via infocmp from file: /home/sys
tem/.terminfo/v/vt100
vt100|vt100-am|dec vt100 (w/advanced video),
        am, msgr, xenl, xon,
        cols#80, it#8, lines#24, vt#3,
        acsc="aaffggjjkkllmmnnooppqqrrssttuuvvwwxxyyzz
{{||}}~~,
        bel=^G, blink=\E[5m$, bold=\E[1m$,
        clear=\E[H\E[J$2, cr=^M, csr=\E[%i%p1%d;%p2%dr,
        cub=\E[%p1%dD, cub1=^H, cud=\E[%p1%dB, cud1=^J,
        cuf=\E[%p1%dC, cuf1=\E[C$,
        cup=\E[%i%p1%d;%p2%dH$, cuu=\E[%p1%dA,
        cuu1=\E[A$, ed=\E[J$2, el=\E[K$,
        el1=\E[1K$, enacs=\E(B\E)0, home=\E[H, ht=^I,
        hts=\EH, ind=^J, ka1=\EOq, ka3=\EOs, kb2=\EOr,
        kbs=^H, kc1=\EOp, kc3=\EOn, kcub1=\EOD,
        kcud1=\EOB,
        kcuf1=\EOC, kcuu1=\EOA, kent=\EOM, kf0=\EOy,
        kf1=\EOP, kf10=\EOx, kf2=\EOQ, kf3=\EOR, kf4=\
EOS,
        kf5=\EOt, kf6=\EOu, kf7=\EOv, kf8=\EOl, kf9=\
EOw,
        rc=\E8, rev=\E[7m$, ri=\EM$, rmacs=^O,
        rmam=\E[?7l, rmkx=\E[?1l\E, rmso=\E[m$,
        rmul=\E[m$,
        rs2=\E\E[?3l\E[?4l\E[?5l\E[?7h\E[?8h, sc=\E7,
        sgr=\E[0%?%p1%p6%|%t;1%;%?%p2%t;4%;%?%p1%p3%|
%t;7%;%?%p4%t;5%;m%?%p9%t\0 16%e\017%;,
        sgr0=\E[m\017$, smacs=^N, smam=\E[?7h,
        smkx=\E[?1h\E=, smso=\E[7m$, smul=\E[4m$,
        tbc=\E[3g,
```

Many options are offered by **infocmp** but they are used very infrequently. As mentioned above, the principal use of this command is to extract a terminal definition in order to modify it so that it corresponds to a new terminal. The modified source definition is then re-inserted into the database after being re-compiled by the **tic** command.

6. The tic command

The **tic** utility allows you to compile a source file that contains terminal characteristics. You can create the source file directly with a text editor. Alternatively, you can modify a file that you have decompiled from an existing object file using the **infocmp** utility. The result of the compilation is a file whose name is extracted from the definition itself. This file is then automatically inserted into the /usr/share/terminfo database. The file is placed in the subdirectory with the same name as the first letter of the file name.

```
# infocmp vt100   vt100-gen
# tic -v vt100-gen
Starting 'vt100|vt100-am|dec vt100 (w/advanced
video)'
Created v/vt100
Linked v/vt100-am
```

Here are two of the most commonly used options of the **tic** command:

-c Carries out an error check on the file specified as an argument. Any errors found are displayed. No compilation is done.

-v[n] Displays (verbose) information on the progress made by **tic**. The n argument is an integer from 1 to 10. It specifies the amount of information to be displayed. The higher this number, the more information is output.

Chapter 10

Time and time zone management

A.	**Clock management: clock, date**	**190**
	1. The software clock	191
	2. The hardware clock	193
B.	**Time zone management**	**193**

kernel version 2.0 to 2.2

On Unix systems, time management is based on the number of seconds elapsed since 00:00 GMT on January 1, 1970. The term **epoch** is used to refer to this year (in reality this is the first year in the epoch covered). At present the Linux kernel stores times in 32-bit variables. More precisely, the number is stored on 31 bits. Because of this the limit date is not the year 2000, but the year 2038!

In addition, the system also manages time zones.

A. Clock management: **clock, date**

Linux has two clocks, a **hardware clock** and a **software clock**. The hardware clock is also called a CMOS clock, after the hardware component used to store the time. The software clock is initialized upon each system boot. These clocks are managed using two commands:

- **clock** for the hardware clock and the software clock,
- **date** for the software clock.

> The **clock** command is gradually being replaced by the **hwclock** command. **hwclock** functions in the same way as **clock**, but has different option names. Nevertheless, **hwclock** accepts the option names used by **clock** for forward compatibility reasons. In addition, **clock** is generally a link to **hwclock**, so as to promote a smooth transition between the two commands.

The hardware clock and the software clock are closely dependent on each other:
- the software clock is initialized automatically on system boot using the hardware clock,
- the hardware clock can be set manually using the software clock.

1. The software clock

Setting

The software clock is set using the **clock -s** command. This command is included in one of the system initialization scripts (*/etc/rc.d/rc.sysinit* for a Redhat distribution or */etc/rc.d/local* for a Slackware distribution). The hardware clock can keep either local time or coordinated universal time (UTC). If you have chosen to keep your clock in UTC you must indicate this to **clock** by specifying the -u option. This tells Linux that it must apply the necessary time difference so as to convert to local time.

Viewing

The **date** command displays the system date and time. The contents and format of this display can be varied by specifying one or more of the options offered by this command. It also depends on the contents of the **LANG** environment variable.

Re-setting

The **date** command also allows you to re-set the system date and time. To do this you must specify the new value in the following format:

MMDDhhmm[[CC]YY][.ss]

where:

MM	specifies the month,
DD	specifies the day of the month,
hh	specifies the hour of the day,
mm	specifies the number of minutes in the hour,
CC	specifies the century (for example 20 for the year 2001),
YY	specifies the year (for example 01 for the year 2001),
ss	specifies the number of seconds in the minute.

As indicated above, the last three values are optional.

In the following example, the system time is set to 12:00 on April 14:

```
# date 04141200
```

It must be noted that only the system administrator is allowed to modify system date and time.

2. The hardware clock

The **clock -w** command sets the hardware clock to the current system time.

Again, if you use UTC you must specify the -u option (cf. the Setting paragraph in the previous sub-section of this chapter entitled "The software clock").

The **clock -r** command displays the contents of the hardware clock.

B. Time zone management

Several time zone management systems have been used by Unix. Linux has adopted a system that is independent from the kernel. This system is based on the /etc/localtime file. This file contains items that describe time difference rules, not only with respect to time zones, but also for changing between winter time and summer time.

This /etc/localtime file is generally a symbolic link to the current time zone file that is stored in the /usr/lib/zoneinfo directory. This directory contains description files for a large number of time zones. These files are object files that have been compiled from source files using the **zic** utility (Zone Info Compiler).

You can view the contents of these files using the **zdump** utility.

Here is an example extract from the /etc/localtime file.

```
# zdump -v /etc/localtime
...
localtime  Sun Mar 30 00:59:59 1997 GMT = Sun Mar 30 01:59:59 1997
MET isdst=0
localtime  Sun Mar 30 01:00:00 1997 GMT = Sun Mar 30 03:00:00 1997
MET DST isdst=1
localtime  Sun Oct 26 00:59:59 1997 GMT = Sun Oct 26 02:59:59 1997
MET DST isdst=1
localtime  Sun Oct 26 01:00:00 1997 GMT = Sun Oct 26 02:00:00 1997
MET isdst=0
localtime  Sun Mar 29 00:59:59 1998 GMT = Sun Mar 29 01:59:59 1998
MET isdst=0
localtime  Sun Mar 29 01:00:00 1998 GMT = Sun Mar 29 03:00:00 1998
MET DST isdst=1
localtime  Sun Oct 25 00:59:59 1998 GMT = Sun Oct 25 02:59:59 1998
MET DST isdst=1
localtime  Sun Oct 25 01:00:00 1998 GMT = Sun Oct 25 02:00:00 1998
MET isdst=0
localtime  Sun Mar 28 00:59:59 1999 GMT = Sun Mar 28 01:59:59 1999
MET isdst=0
localtime  Sun Mar 28 01:00:00 1999 GMT = Sun Mar 28 03:00:00 1999
MET DST isdst=1
localtime  Sun Oct 31 00:59:59 1999 GMT = Sun Oct 31 02:59:59 1999
MET DST isdst=1
localtime  Sun Oct 31 01:00:00 1999 GMT = Sun Oct 31 02:00:00 1999
MET isdst=0
...
```

To view a specific time zone, you can indicate the time zone instead of the file name. For example, the information in the above example could have been produced by calling **zdump** as follows: zdump -v MET. The MET zone in this example refers to Medium European Time. The **date** command tells you which time zone your system is in, as in the following example:

```
$ date
Mon Oct 26 10:47:21 MET 1998
```

If you call this command when summer time is in operation, the abbreviation DST (Daylight Saving Time) appears to indicate this:

```
$ date
Thu Oct 08 04:25:00 MET DST 1998
```

Configuring the timezone system

To enable Linux to manage the various time changes, the time change rules must be defined. Here is an example of the steps you can follow to define time change rules:

- cd /usr/lib/zoneinfo
- cp MET localtime
- ln -sf localtime posixrules.

Having followed this sequence, you now need to ask the system to apply the rules contained in the /usr/lib/zoneinfo/localtime file. You can use the **clock** command for this purpose. This is because time change rules are applied when the time is set or reset. As mentioned earlier in this chapter, time can be stored in local time or in UTC (UTC is in fact the same as GMT: Greenwich Mean Time). The options you use will depend on how time is stored in the hardware clock of your machine:

- The hardware clock of your machine stores in UTC: In this case you must call the **clock** command as follows: **clock -u -s**. The -s option asks the system to set the hardware clock using the contents of the software clock. The -u option indicates that the hardware clock stores time in UTC.

- The hardware clock of your machine stores in local time: In this case you must specify the -s option alone. In this mode however, a time change will be applied automatically only if your machine is up and running at the moment the time change is due to occur. If this is not the case, you must update the clock manually. To do this you can call the **clock** command in the following form: **clock -w**. Alternatively, you can reset the BIOS upon system startup.

The first mode is clearly preferable to the second. However, the second mode must be used if Linux is not the only operating system on your machine. The clock must be managed by one system only, in order to avoid accumulation of time errors.

Chapter 11

System accounting

A.	Current sessions: **who**	**200**
B.	History of user sessions: **last**	**202**
C.	Reporting on user connection time: **ac**	**205**
D.	Activating and de-activating process accounting: **accton**	**206**
E.	Structure of the process accounting records .	**207**
F.	Using accounting information: **lastcomm, sa**	**209**
	1. The **lastcomm** command	**209**
	2. The **sa** command	**211**

kernel version 2.0 to 2.2

Unix systems in general, and Linux systems in particular have a set of utilities that provide statistics on system usage:

who	Shows who is currently logged in.
last	Shows all users who have logged in, previously or currently.
ac	Provides a report on the duration of user sessions, by day and by user.
lastcomm	Provides a history of commands executed on the system.
sa	Provides statistics on executed commands.

These utilities use various files that are managed by the kernel:

/var/adm/utmp	Contains information on current connections to the system. This file is used by the **who** command.
/var/adm/wtmp	Contains information on past and current connections to the system. This file is used by the **last** and **ac** commands.
/var/account/pacct	Contains information on processes that have been executed on the system. This file is used by the **lastcomm** and **sa** commands.

Chapter 11

The first two of these files are managed automatically by the kernel. In contrast to these files, the management of the /var/account/pacct file is not activated by default. This file is used for process accounting purposes. It contains a trace of commands executed on the system and can be used to generate statistics on the usage of the system. As we shall see later, a certain amount of information is logged for each command that is executed. This mechanism is not a sub-system but it is managed directly by the kernel that uses the **acct**(2) function for this purpose.

This mechanism does not operate by default. It must be activated using the **accton** command. When process accounting is switched on, the kernel will create a record in the /var/account/pacct file for each process that runs. As large numbers of processes run on most systems, this file can grow quickly and may even saturate the file system in which it is installed. When this happens, the process accounting mechanism is switched off automatically until disk space becomes available.

It must be noted that Linux uses BSD type process accounting. This mechanism originated with Unix version 7.

> *The Linux accounting utilities are also used by AIX, Digital Unix, HPUX and SunOS systems. System V accounting uses different utilities but is based on the same data structure.*

Most of the Linux accounting utilities are part of the GNUacct6.3.2 software suite.

> *The newer versions of these utilities are more compatible with the BSD standard. When you install these new versions on Linux 2.2.x, you have to recompile them.*

kernel version 2.0 to 2.2

These process accounting utilities will be covered later on in this chapter. First, we will describe the utilities that provide information on user sessions, both past and current.

A. Current sessions: **who**

Information on current user sessions is stored in the */var/run/utmp* file. You may have a link to this file from */var/adm/utmp* or from */var/log/utmp*. The file is deleted and recreated on each system boot. This is done from one of the initialization scripts (*/etc/rc.d/rc.sysinit* for a Redhat distribution or */etc/rc.d/local* for a Slackware distribution).

The */var/run/utmp* file is managed by the **login** process when the user logs in and by the **init** process when the user logs out. **login** stores information about the session that has just opened and **init** writes the time at which the session finished.

The structure of the */var/run/utmp* file is defined by the */usr/include/utmp.h* file. Here is an extract from this file:

```
struct utmp
{
   short    ut_type;        /* type of login */
   pid_t    ut_pid;         /* pid of login-process */
   char     ut_line[UT_LINESIZE];  /* devicename of tty */
   char     ut_id[4];       /* inittab id */
   time_t   ut_time;        /* login time */
   char     ut_user[UT_NAMESIZE];  /* username, not null-term */
   char     ut_host[UT_HOSTSIZE];  /* hostname for remote login.. */
   long     ut_addr;        /* IP addr of remote host */
};
```

This file is read by the **who** command. **who** provides information on the users that are currently logged into the system. Here are some examples of this command:

```
[78]-system(merlin)~: who
system    tty6      Jan 29 09:12
system    ttyp0     Jan 30 12:49 (:0.0)
root      ttyp1     Jan 30 12:49 (:0.0)
soloa     ttyp2     Jan 30 17:09 (morgan.dorset)
[79]-system(merlin)~: who -H
USER      LINE      LOGIN-TIME   FROM
system    tty6      Jan 29 09:12
system    ttyp0     Jan 30 12:49 (:0.0)
root      ttyp1     Jan 30 12:49 (:0.0)
soloa     ttyp2     Jan 30 17:09 (morgan.dorset)
[80]-system(merlin)~:who -u
system    tty6      Jan 29 09:12   old
system    ttyp0     Jan 30 12:49        .       (:0.0)
root      ttyp1     Jan 30 12:49 01:17  (:0.0)
soloa     ttyp2     Jan 30 17:09 10:01  (morgan.dorset)
[81]-system(merlin)~:who -m
merlin!system   ttyp0      Jan 30 12:49 (:0.0)
[82]-system(merlin)~:who am i
merlin!system   ttyp0      Jan 30 12:49 (:0.0)
```

Here are the options that are most commonly used with this command:

- -H Displays column headings.
- -u Displays the amount of time the user has been idle. A dot (.) means that the user has been idle for less than a minute. The term 'old' indicates that the user has been idle for over 24 hours.
- -w Indicates whether or not the user accepts messages that are sent by the **write** utility. A plus sign (+) indicates that the user accepts **write** messages. A minus sign (-) indicates that the user does not accept **write** messages.
- -m Displays information only for the user who called the command. This is equivalent to the **who am i** command.

B. History of user sessions: last

While the /var/run/utmp file stores information on the current sessions, the /var/adm/wtmp file stores information on the sessions that have terminated. The same information is written to both of these files except that it is written twice to /var/adm/wtmp: it is written once when the user logs in, and a second time when the user logs out.

Unlike *utmp*, the *wtmp* file is not created automatically. It must be created by the system administrator. As this file contains information on all the user sessions that take place on the system, it can become very large, rapidly. Consequently, the system administrator must purge the file regularly.

As with *utmp*, you cannot access *wtmp* directly. The **last** utility is provided for this purpose.

When called without options or arguments, **last** displays the contents of the /var/adm/wtmp file. Depending on the size of this file, this display may take some time.

By default, **last** displays the following information:

- user name,
- terminal name (without the /dev/ prefix),
- if the login was made from a remote machine, the name of the remote machine or its IP address is displayed. In the case of a pseudo terminal of a graphical session, this field indicates the terminal and the screen in the **:terminal.screen** format.
- date and time of the start of the session,
- time of the end of the session,
- duration of the session.

Chapter 11

The last line of the /var/adm/wtmp file contains the creation date of this file. The following command allows you to display this information by itself:

```
[44]-system(merlin)~:last -y | tail -1
wtmp begins Tue Sep 16 1998 22:40
```

The `-y` option displays the years concerned (these are not displayed by default).

The **last** command allows you to specify arguments that limit the display of wtmp lines to those that correspond to a certain criteria. **last** output is more readily useable when the command is called in this way.

For this purpose you can specify:

– terminal names
– user names.

Terminal names must be specified without the /dev/ prefix. However, you can specify them with or without the tty prefix.

You can specify several arguments. These can be terminal names and/or user names. In this case **last** will display those lines that contain at least one of the arguments specified. Your request then, will be interpreted as a logical (inclusive) OR as the following example illustrates:

```
[45]-system(merlin)~:last root ttyp3 | head
system   ttyp3   arthur.dorset.   Mon May  3 17:39 - 21:11  (03:32)
root     tty3                     Mon Apr 19 13:40 - 13:41  (00:00)
system   ttyp3   :0.0             Wed Apr 14 16:12 - 13:14  (4+21:02)
system   ttyp3   morgan.dorset.   Sat Apr 10 14:04 - 14:06  (00:01)
system   ttyp3   :0.0             Fri Apr  9 09:44 - 09:48  (00:04)
system   ttyp3   morgan.dorset.   Thu Apr  8 21:08 - 22:06  (00:57)
system   ttyp3   morgan.dorset.   Thu Apr  8 19:45 - 20:03  (00:18)
system   ttyp3   :0.0             Sun Mar 28 21:30 - 21:34  (00:04)
root     ttyp1   merlin:0.0       Mon Mar 22 20:50 - down   (00:00)
system   ttyp3   :0.0             Sat Mar 20 14:24 - 14:34  (00:10)
```

System accounting

kernel version 2.0 to 2.2

Two special names appear amongst the user names. These are *shutdown* and *reboot*. Records beginning with these names show when the system was stopped, and when the system was restarted. Here is a command that tells you when the system was last stopped and when it was last started:

```
[46]-system(merlin)~:last shutdown reboot | head -2
reboot     system boot                    Fri Apr 30 22:34
shutdown system down                      Thu Apr 29 20:31
```

The */var/adm/wtmp* file contains further information that you can view by calling **last** using other options:

- `-a` Displays all the file records.
- `-s` Displays times, with seconds indicated.
- `-x` Displays changes in runlevel ('runlevel' is indicated as a special user name). This option also displays shutdown records.

*If **last** is interrupted by a SIGINT signal, it indicates the line it was currently processing before it was exits.*

```
[53]-system(merlin)~:last
system    ttyp2     arthur.dorset.  Tue May  4 10:12    still logged in
system    ftp       arthur.dorset.  Tue May  4 10:10 - 10:15  (00:05)
system    ttyp3     arthur.dorset.  Mon May  3 17:39 - 21:11  (03:32)
...
system    ttyp1     :0.0            Thu Apr  1 19:20 - 19:21  (00:00)
system    ttyp0     :0.0            Thu Apr  1 19:20 - 22:00  (02:40)
system    ttyp0     :0.0            Thu Aug  6 13:02 - 13:23  (00:20)

interrupted at Thu Aug  6 13:02
```

LINUX Administration

C. Reporting on user connection time: ac

In common with **last**, the **ac** utility uses the /var/adm/wtmp file. When called without argument or option, **ac** displays the total length of time that all the users have been connected to the system. If you indicate one or several user names as arguments, **ac** displays the total amount of time that the specified user(s) have been logged in.

You can display these statistics by user and/or by day. If you request this information by day, **ac** will display it for each day covered by the /var/adm/wtmp file.

Here are a few examples of the use of this utility:

```
[merlin]# ac
        total     6488.00
[merlin]# ac root
        total       72.43
[merlin]# ac -p
        squid        0.00
        sgbd       138.65
        ftp          2.02
        webroot    118.00
        grass        1.22
        root        72.43
        soloa       32.53
        solob      191.33
        system    5857.39
        total     6413.18
[merlin]# ac -d|head -5
Sep 16  total        1.99
Sep 17  total       16.51
Sep 18  total        0.38
Sep 19  total        4.67
Sep 21  total        7.51
[merlin]# ac -d|tail -5
Apr 29  total        2.63
Apr 30  total        2.83
May  1  total       48.02
May  2  total       48.50
Today   total       42.24
[merlin]# ac -d -p|tail -5
        system      48.50
May  2  total       48.50
        soloa        0.02
        system      42.23
Today   total       42.25
```

As a user can open several sessions (on several serial terminals, using telnet or on several X windows) it is quite possible for a user's connection time to exceed 24 hours for the same day.

D. Activating and de-activating process accounting: **accton**

By default, process accounting is not active. In addition, the accounting utilities may not even be included in your distribution. In this case you can install them from the GNUacct6.3.2 software suite.

To activate process accounting, you must call the **accton** command, supplying the name of the accounting file as an argument. This file is generally */var/account/pact*. This is usually the default name used by the accounting utilities, although you can rename this file if you want to.

If you wish to activate process accounting automatically on system startup, you can add the following lines to one of the initialization scripts:

```
if [ -f /var/account/pacct ]; then
    /usr/sbin/accton /var/account/pacct
    echo 'Starting account'>/dev/console
fi
```

> You must create the accounting file manually as the accounting utilities do not create it automatically. If the file does not exist, the kernel continues to call the **acct(2)** function without being able to store the records it generates.

To deactivate process accounting you must call the **accton** command without arguments. It must be noted that this is the only way to switch off this mechanism.

E. Structure of the process accounting records

This structure is defined in the standard Unix file */usr/include/sys/act.h*. On Linux systems installed with **libc5**, this file is combined with another file called */usr/include/linux/acct.h*. On the other hand, **libc6** uses */usr/include/linux/acct.h* as a standalone file. This is in common with the **libc6** philosophy of greater independence from the system.

However, the **libc6** version of */usr/include/linux/acct.h* does not have as rich a structure as that supplied with Linux kernel 2.2.0. In addition, the **sa** command does not have its full range of options when used with **libc6**. This is because the compilation of the **sa** command depends on the structure of the accounting file and the compile options for this command have to be modified accordingly.

kernel version 2.0 to 2.2

/usr/include/linux/acct.h records contain the following fields:
- command name (regrettably, without any arguments),
- CPU time: system time plus user time,
- total time that elapsed between the start and the end of the process,
- date on which the process was started,
- UID and GID of the process,
- terminal controlling the process,
- average amount of memory used,
- number of characters read and written,
- number of blocks read and written,
- minimum number of page faults,
- maximum number of page faults,
- number of swaps,
- return code,
- flags.

F. Using accounting information: lastcomm, sa

1. The lastcomm command

lastcomm displays information on commands that have been executed on your system. By default, this command lists information on all commands, starting from the one that was executed most recently. This information is displayed in six columns:

– process name,
– flags that were recorded by system accounting routines. These can be the following:
  - **S**   The command was executed by root (**S** for super user).
  - **F**   The command was executed by a fork but without an *exec*.
  - **C**   The command was executed in PDP11 compatibility mode (this is not used on Linux).
  - **D**   The command generated a core file when it terminated.
  - **X**   The command terminated after receiving a SIGTERM signal.
– name of the user that started the command,
– terminal that controlled the process (if no terminal was associated with this process the **??** characters are displayed),
– total execution time,
– date and time the process terminated.

Here is an example of the use of the **lastcomm** command:

```
[merlin]# lastcomm|head
sh          S     root   ??       0.01 secs Mon May  3 17:35
atrun       S     root   ??       0.01 secs Mon May  3 17:35
sendmail    SF    root   ??       0.00 secs Mon May  3 17:34
more              root   stderr   0.03 secs Mon May  3 17:32
ftp               root   stderr   0.00 secs Mon May  3 17:31
bash        F     root   stderr   0.00 secs Mon May  3 17:31
bash        F     root   stderr   0.00 secs Mon May  3 17:31
more              root   stderr   0.01 secs Mon May  3 17:31
sh          S     root   ??       0.01 secs Mon May  3 17:30
atrun       S     root   ??       0.01 secs Mon May  3 17:30
```

Interpreting the results of the **lastcomm** command can be quite complex. One reason for this is that command options and arguments are not displayed. In addition, a command executed by a user can call other commands, which also appear in the list. A typical example of this, is the **man** command, which calls **groff**, **troff** and **grotty**:

```
[merlin]# lastcomm|head
gunzip            root     stderr   0.01 secs Mon May  3 17:39
lastcomm    X     root     stderr   0.10 secs Mon May  3 17:39
head              root     stderr   0.01 secs Mon May  3 17:39
gunzip            system   ttyp3    0.01 secs Mon May  3 17:39
sh                system   ttyp3    0.02 secs Mon May  3 17:39
sh                system   ttyp3    0.00 secs Mon May  3 17:39
gzip              system   ttyp3    0.03 secs Mon May  3 17:39
groff             system   ttyp3    0.03 secs Mon May  3 17:39
troff             system   ttyp3    0.25 secs Mon May  3 17:39
grotty            system   ttyp3    0.06 secs Mon May  3 17:39
```

You can restrict the display to the lines concerning a specific process, user or terminal. You can specify several of these arguments (process(es), user(s) and/or terminal(s)). In this case, **lastcomm** will display those lines that contain at least one of the arguments specified. Your request then, will be interpreted as a logical (inclusive) OR. For example, the `lastcomm ttyp3 bash soloa` command will display the lines concerning the processes called bash, and the processes started by soloa, and the processes controlled by `ttyp3`.

It must be remembered that these fields are filled in by accounting functions when the processes have terminated. The sixth field shows the date and time that these processes terminated and the commands are listed in the inverse order of this termination time. This order is not necessarily the same as the order in which these processes were started. A process can be started before another process, and appear in the **lastcomm** list later than the second process. This is simply because it terminated after the second process.

Further information on executed processes can be obtained using the **sa** command.

2. The sa command

For each command executed, the **sa** command displays execution time and system resources consumed.

When called without options this command displays the following result:

```
[merlin]# sa|head
 1156175 12872073.21re 12903691.25cp     295avio      258k
     356  5684402.58re  6394008.39cp  956748avio      209k  ***other*
     121  3860157.39re  6374678.55cp       0avio    11058k
       7   133366.93re   133267.64cp       0avio    11360k
   24452      543.33re      485.13cp       0avio      765k  ccl
      92    69396.34re      251.90cp       0avio     2118k  X
     223    17506.63re      109.84cp       0avio     2932k  netscape
   29251      288.82re       84.28cp       0avio      302k  cpp
     361       71.90re       66.05cp       0avio     1278k  latex
      99    46648.76re       59.01cp       0avio     1324k  lyx
```

The first line displays the column totals.

kernel version 2.0 to 2.2

The results are displayed in six columns. The last column shows the name of the command or process. The first column shows the number of times the command or the process has been run. The other columns are identified by codes that are suffixed to the values contained in the columns. These codes have the following signification:

- **re**   Total execution time.
- **cp**   CPU time (sum of system mode time and user mode time).
- **avio**   Average number of input/output operations per execution.
- **k**   Average amount of core memory used with respect to CPU time (in kilobytes).

You can specify a number of options to display other values:

- **k*sec**   Total memory used in kilo-core seconds (obtained using the -k option).
- **tio**   Total number of input/output operations (obtained using the -D option).
- **s**   CPU system time in seconds (obtained using the -l option).
- **u**   CPU user time in seconds (obtained using the -l option).

The **sa** command offers a wide range of options. Some of these options change what is displayed in the different columns. Other options allow you to sort the display according to values contained in specific columns.

Here is a selection of the options that allow you to sort the display:

- **-b**   Sorts the display according to the sum of system and user time divided by the number of executions.

-d Sorts the display according to the average number of input/output operations to and from disk.

-D Sorts the display according to the total number of input/output operations to and from disk.

-k Sorts the display according to the average memory usage with respect to CPU time.

-K Sorts the display according to the total memory usage.

-n Sorts the display according to the number of executions (this is the default criterion).

Here is a selection of options that allow you to specify other functionalities:

-a Displays explicitly any commands that have been executed only once and those with names containing unprintable characters. By default, these commands are grouped together in a line marked as ***other*.

-c Total time, system time and user time values are also displayed as percentages.

-i Information contained in the accounting summary files is not taken into account.

-m Displays information user by user (rather than process by process).

-s Creation or update of accounting sum-mary files:
– /var/account/savacct for results by process,
– /var/account/usracct for results by user.

kernel version 2.0 to 2.2

Updating these two summary files allows you to reinitialize the /var/account/pacct file. This technique prevents this accounting file from growing indefinitely. Here is a simple method of reinitializing this file:

`# accton`	Deactivate process accounting.
`# sa -s`	Update the accounting summary files.
`# >| /var/account/pacct`	Reinitialize the accounting file.
`# accton /var/account/pacct`	Reactivate process accounting.

> *This operation can be carried out automatically. For systems that are stopped and restarted frequently, this sequence can be included in an initialization script. For systems that operate continuously, such as servers, this can be implemented periodically by the **cron** daemon.*

> *After you have updated the summary files, you must delete the contents of the accounting file so that this information will not be used twice by **sa**. If you do not do this, you must specify the -i option so that **sa** will use only the accounting file and will not take the summary files into account.*

Chapter 12

Rebuilding the kernel

A. In which circumstances? **216**

B. How? **217**
    1. Updating the kernel source code **217**
    2. Compiling the kernel **218**

C. Loadable modules **220**
    1. Preparing the kernel **221**
    2. Compiling and installing the loadable modules . **222**
    3. Using loadable modules **223**

kernel version 2.0 to 2.2

One of the great advantages of Linux is that it is supplied with the source code. This is a characteristic that Linux shares with other freely available systems such as FreeBSD. This means that, anyone can propose a solution to a problem, or suggest an improvement to the kernel. Because of this, there were 80 software development specialists working on Linux kernel versions 1.x.x. For the 2.x.x versions, this figure has grown to 190. This effort has resulted in rapid technical development, and an increasingly powerful and stable kernel.

In addition, Linux has always been closely linked with the Internet. Because of this, a patch or an update to solve a problem is often available only a few days after the development team has been informed of the problem. This was notably the case when a Pentium bug was discovered. In under a week, the Linux kernel had been adapted to counter this bug.

A. In which circumstances?

Sometimes you have to update the version of the Linux kernel. There can be a number of reasons for this:

- to correct problems that have been discovered,
- to improve performance,
- to install one or more drivers for new peripheral devices,
- to use new features (for example the RAID 5 solution that became available with version 2.0.35),
- to update the kernel.

It must be noted that if you have a kernel that fully satisfies its users, it does not have to be updated. Moreover, some versions are noted for their exceptional stability or instability and the stability of a version becomes known only with the passing of time.

B. How?

In order to re-build the kernel, you have to obtain the source files. These are generally available in the form of a file in **tar** format, compressed by **gzip** or **bzip2**.

Once you have obtained this file, you have to decompress it and extract the file hierarchy it contains.

You can do this using the following command (where `dir` is the directory in which you want to install the source file hierarchy):

```
# cd dir

# tar zxvf linux-.2.y.z
```

This command will create a file hierarchy containing all the files necessary to build a kernel. These files will occupy approximately 80 megabytes of disk space.

You are now ready to start configuring and compiling the kernel. First, however, you may wish to update the source code in order to include the latest corrections and/or improvements.

1. Updating the kernel source code

When modifications or corrections have been made to the kernel, a new *linux2.y.z* file is created. The *z* suffix is a number that is incremented each time a new version of this file is made. However, this file is quite bulky (from 10 to 13 megabytes). Consequently, you would not want to download it completely each time it is modified, especially if the modifications made are minor ones. In general therefore, you will obtain the *patch2.y.z+1* file that contains only the modifications that have been made. This file is used to modify your existing source code.

However, you must be careful to respect the version number sequence. If you have obtained the set of source files for the 2.2.x kernel, the only modification file you can apply to this source code is the file entitled *patch2.2.x+1*. Before you can apply any given patch to a kernel source, you must ensure that all the intermediate patches have been applied previously.

Here are the steps you must follow to apply a patch:

- obtain the *patch2.y.z+1* file
- decompress the patch: `gunzip patch-2.y.z+1`
- go to the directory that contains the *linux2.y.z+1* directory (this is generally */usr/src*): `cd /usr/src`
- apply the patch: `patch -p0 <patch-2.y.z+1`
- search for files that could not be updated: `find linux2.y.z name "*.rej"`

If no files were found in the last step, you are now ready to configure and compile the kernel. Any files found in the final step indicate that the patch could not be applied correctly and the source files have not been updated properly. In this case you must repeat this procedure when you have a set of uncorrupted source files.

2. Compiling the kernel

When you compile a kernel, a large number of variables allow you to integrate certain features. In order to set these variables correctly, you can use one of the following commands:

make config	You can use this command in the case of a serial terminal that manages neither colors nor graphics.
make menuconfig	This command is more user-friendly than the previous one. It can be used on a text terminal that manages colors (such as a virtual console).

make xconfig   You can use this command only on an X system. This command is the most user-friendly of the set.

These three commands allow you to configure the compilation phase. The compilation phase itself is implemented in three steps using the following commands:

make dep   Determines the dependencies.

make clean   Deletes the old object files.

make [b]zlilo   Rebuilds a kernel that can be booted from the MBR (master boot record). Alternatively, you can use one of the following commands:

make [b]zdisk   To rebuild a kernel on a bootable floppy disk. The floppy disk must be present in the floppy drive.

make [b]zImage   To rebuild a kernel without specifying a destination. The system administrator must then ensure that it is used upon system boot. One use of this command is to rebuild a kernel for another site.

C. Loadable modules

The more peripheral devices the kernel has to manage, the more disk and memory space it will need. These sizes can make it difficult to create a bootable floppy diskette.

One reason for this increase in size is the presence of the drivers that are necessary to control the peripheral devices. Another reason is the inclusion of programs that provide new features, such as the management of different file systems.

However, there are two ways to include new features into the system: you can do this either statically, or dynamically. **Static** inclusion means that the new features are integrated directly onto the kernel. On the other hand, **dynamic** inclusion results in a set of object modules being created with a **.o** extension to their file names. These modules are not included in the kernel. They are loaded into memory as and when they are needed. One objective of these loadable modules is to minimize the size of the kernel.

Another advantage of this technique is that it allows you to add new peripheral devices without having to recompile the kernel and without having to initialize the system. In addition, you can update a driver or another module without touching the kernel, simply by replacing the file concerned.

1. Preparing the kernel

The management of loadable modules is defined by three variables. In turn, these three variables are defined by the responses to the following three questions, which are generated by the **make config** command:

```
# make config,
...
Loadable module support:
Enable loadable module support (CONFIG_MODULES)
[Y/n/?]
Set version information on all symbols for modules
(CONFIG_MODVERSIONS) [N/y/?]
Kernel daemon support (e.g. autoload of modules)
(CONFIG_KERNELD) [Y/n/?]
```

CONFIG_MODULES	To activate the management of loadable modules.
CONFIG_MODVERSIONS	To specify whether on not the loadable modules used by one kernel version (2.y.) can be used by a later version without being recompiled. However, it is always a good idea to recompile these modules. In this way, you will always work with their latest versions, and you will have the benefit of the corrections and improvements they provide.
CONFIG_KERNELD	To activate automatic loading of loadable modules. Since kernel version 2.2.0, the CONFIG_KERNELD variable has been replaced by the CONFIG_KMOD variable.

All you have to do now is to determine the kernel features that the loadable modules must provide, and rebuild the kernel.

2. Compiling and installing the loadable modules

Compilation of loadable modules is independent of that of the kernel. It is handled by a separate procedure that is run by calling the **make modules** command.

Once the modules have been compiled, they can be installed using the **make modules_install** command.

This command creates the directory */lib/modules/x.y.z*, where *x.y.z* correspond to the version of the kernel. The loadable modules are installed in this directory, either directly or in subdirectories. The following example illustrates this:

```
[20]-system(merlin)/lib/modules:ls 2.0.0/
2.0.32/   2.2.0/   2.2.3/   2.2.5/   2.2.6/   2.2.7/   misc/
[21]-system(merlin)/lib/modules:ls 2.2.5
fs/          misc/          modules.dep   net/
[22]-system(merlin)/lib/modules:cd 2.2.5
[23]-system(merlin)/lib/modules/2.2.5:ls fs misc net
fs:
autofs.o        minix.o              ntfs.o           ufs.o
fat.o           msdos.o              smbfs.o          umsdos.o
hfs.o           nls_iso8859-1.o      sysv.o           vfat.o

misc:
awe_wave.o   sb.o    sound.o    soundcore.o    soundlow.o   uart401.o

net:
bsd_comp.o         dummy.o              eql.o              ppp_deflate.o
```

LINUX Administration

Chapter 12

3. Using loadable modules

When the features provided by a module are required, the module must be loaded into the kernel. This can be done in three ways:

— manually, as required,
— automatically, when the system boots,
— automatically, as and when required.

insmod

To load a module manually, you can call the **insmod** command, indicating the name of the module you wish to load. However, the loading may fail, because some modules depend on other modules. For example, the **vfat** type file system is managed by a loadable module called `vfat.o`. Any attempt to load `vfat.o` alone will fail because this module depends on the `fat.o` module.

Therefore you must load `fat.o` first, and then load `vfat.o`.

```
[merlin]# insmod vfat
/lib/modules/2.2.7/fs/vfat.o: unresolved symbol fat_statfs
/lib/modules/2.2.7/fs/vfat.o: unresolved symbol fat_scan
/lib/modules/2.2.7/fs/vfat.o: unresolved symbol fat_put_inode
/lib/modules/2.2.7/fs/vfat.o: unresolved symbol fat_fs_panic
/lib/modules/2.2.7/fs/vfat.o: unresolved symbol fat_cache_inval_inode
/lib/modules/2.2.7/fs/vfat.o: unresolved symbol fat_delete_inode
/lib/modules/2.2.7/fs/vfat.o: unresolved symbol fat_read_inode
/lib/modules/2.2.7/fs/vfat.o: unresolved symbol fat_mark_buffer_dirty
/lib/modules/2.2.7/fs/vfat.o: unresolved symbol fat_add_cluster
/lib/modules/2.2.7/fs/vfat.o: unresolved symbol fat_notify_change
/lib/modules/2.2.7/fs/vfat.o: unresolved symbol fat_write_inode
/lib/modules/2.2.7/fs/vfat.o: unresolved symbol fat_date_unix2dos
/lib/modules/2.2.7/fs/vfat.o: unresolved symbol fat_get_entry
/lib/modules/2.2.7/fs/vfat.o: unresolved symbol fat_esc2uni
/lib/modules/2.2.7/fs/vfat.o: unresolved symbol fat_readdirx
/lib/modules/2.2.7/fs/vfat.o: unresolved symbol fat_put_super
/lib/modules/2.2.7/fs/vfat.o: unresolved symbol fat_brelse
/lib/modules/2.2.7/fs/vfat.o: unresolved symbol fat_lock_creation
/lib/modules/2.2.7/fs/vfat.o: unresolved symbol fat_unlock_creation
/lib/modules/2.2.7/fs/vfat.o: unresolved symbol fat_dir_operations
/lib/modules/2.2.7/fs/vfat.o: unresolved symbol fat_read_super
[merlin]# echo $?
1[merlin]# insmod fat
[merlin]# insmod vfat
[merlin]# echo $?
0
```

Loading modules manually using **insmod** can be a problem if you do not know how the modules depend on one another. However, this was the only way of loading modules before kernel version 2.0. With this version, the **depmod** and **modprobe** utilities appeared. **depmod** builds the table of dependencies between modules and **modprobe** loads a module along with all the other modules on which it depends. These utilities also allow you to load modules automatically.

Listing loaded modules: lsmod

The **lsmod** command displays information on all loaded modules:

```
[merlin]# lsmod
Module            Size    Used by
vfat              11064   0   (unused)
fat               23912   0   [vfat]
```

All this command does, is to format the information contained in the /proc/modules file. This information is displayed in four columns:

- **Module** — Shows the names of the different modules.
- **Size** — Shows the size of each module.
- **Used** — Indicates how many processes are currently using the module. If the module is used directly by the kernel, this field is blank.
- **by** — Can contain various pieces of information:
  - **(unused)** — Indicates that the module is not being used at present. If the module is used directly by the kernel, this field is blank.

[name]   Indicates that the "name" module is dependent on the module concerned.

(autoclean)   Is a flag that marks this module for the **kerneld** process.

Constructing the dependencies table: depmod

The table of dependencies is constructed using the **/sbin/depmod -a** command.

As a general rule, this command is called automatically upon system boot from an initialization script (*/etc/rc.d/rc.sysinit* for a Redhat distribution or */etc/rc.d/rc.modules* for a Slackware distribution).

This command creates the */lib/modules/x.y.z/modules.dep* file, where *x.y.z* corresponds to the kernel version number.

This file lists the modules that the kernel can use, along with their dependencies:

```
[merlin]# cat modules.dep
/lib/modules/2.2.5/fs/autofs.o:

/lib/modules/2.2.5/fs/fat.o:

/lib/modules/2.2.5/fs/hfs.o:

/lib/modules/2.2.5/fs/minix.o:

/lib/modules/2.2.5/fs/msdos.o: /lib/modules/2.2.5/fs/fat.o

/lib/modules/2.2.5/fs/nls_iso8859-1.o:

/lib/modules/2.2.5/fs/sysv.o:

/lib/modules/2.2.5/fs/ufs.o:

/lib/modules/2.2.5/fs/umsdos.o: /lib/modules/2.2.5/fs/fat.o
/lib/modules/2.2.5/fs/msdos.o

/lib/modules/2.2.5/fs/vfat.o:     /lib/modules/2.2.5/fs/fat.o
```

Rebuilding the kernel

kernel version 2.0 to 2.2

This dependencies table is used by the **modprobe** command.

modprobe

The **modprobe** command loads a module along with all the modules on which it depends. To do this, it uses the /lib/modules/x.y.z/modules.dep file (this file must previously have been created or updated by the **depmod** command):

```
[merlin]# ls
fs/           misc/          modules.dep    net/
[merlin]# ls -lu modules.dep
-rw-r--r--   1 root     root        1115 May   3 13:14 modules.dep
[merlin]# date
Mon May  3 13:31:46 MET DST 1999
[merlin]# modprobe vfat
[merlin]# ls -lu modules.dep
-rw-r--r--   1 root     root        1115 May   3 13:31 modules.dep
[merlin]# lsmod
Module                  Size   Used by
vfat                    11064  0   (unused)
fat                     23912  0   [vfat]
```

This command allows you to load modules automatically. You can include this command in an initialization script in order to load a certain number of modules and their dependent modules, upon system boot. Alternatively this command can be called automatically, as and when necessary.

Automatic loading upon system boot

You can use **modprobe** to load a certain number of modules upon system boot, without having to worry about any possible dependencies. To this end you can call this command from an initialization script (/etc/rc.d/rc.sysinit for a Redhat distribution or /etc/rc.d/rc.modules for a Slackware distribution).

Automatic loading as and when required

Another purpose of **modprobe** is to provide a means of loading modules automatically, as and when the kernel requires them.

Originally, this technique was implemented by the **kerneld** process, which acted as an intermediary between the kernel and the **modprobe** command. Communications between the kernel and the **kerneld** process took place using the IPC (Inter Process Communication) mechanism. This meant that the kernel had to be configured to manage IPC's.

The **kerneld** process must be started as soon as possible after **depmod** has set up the dependencies table.

Using **kerneld** has two drawbacks:
- **kerneld** runs in user mode and is therefore interruptible. This can stop modules being loaded and prevent the correct functioning of the kernel.
- **kerneld** and the kernel communicate via IPCs. This is not an ideal solution.

As of kernel version 2.2, an alternative to **kerneld** is offered by a kernel thread called **kmod**. This mechanism functions quicker and avoids using IPCs.

For the present (up to version 2.2.5 of the kernel), **kmod** can only load the modules. It cannot unload them after a certain idle time, as **kerneld** can. However, you can remedy this deficiency by calling periodically the **rmmod -a** command (for example using the **cron** daemon).

Unloading a module: rmmod

You can unload a module by calling the **rmmod** command, and supplying the name of the module you want to unload.

You can also ask **rmmod** to unload only unused modules and/or those on which no other module depends. To do this, you can call **rmmod** specifying the -a option.

It must be noted that you can also unload a module using the **modprobe -r** command. Moreover, this command uses the table of dependencies to unload any modules on which the specified module depends, provided that these modules are not being used.

Index

!

/etc/securetty
    administration access restriction, *91*
/etc/login.defs, *34*
/etc/motd, *95*
/etc/rc, *20*
/etc/rc.local, *20*
/etc/securetty, *91*
/etc/usertty, *91*
    general access restriction, *91*
/sbin/depmod, *225*
/usr/share/terminfo, *184*
/var/adm/utmp, *200*
/var/log/utmp, *200*
/var/spool/cron, *20*
See also file

A

ac, *198*, *205*
    reporting on user connection time, *205*
accton, *199*
    activating/de-activating
    process accounting, *206*
agetty, *176*
AIX, *28*, *32*, *160*, *199*
also, *98*
Apple Macintosh, *42*
archiving
    local files, *130*
    remote files on the local tape device, *131*
ASCII, *119*
at, *89*
AT&T, *11*, *106*
automatic loading
    as and when required, *227*
    upon system boot, *226*

B

badblocks, *54*
bash, *75*, *93*, *147*
BIOS, *18*, *196*

block group descriptor, *50*
blocks bitmap, *46*
boot
    process, *18*
    prompt, *22*
BSD, *19 - 20, 28, 32, 44, 84 - 85, 95, 106, 135, 151, 160, 181*
BUFSIZ, *163*
bzip2, *217*

C

cd, *218*
clock management, *190*
    clock, date, *190*
    CMOS clock, *190*
    hardware clock, *190*
    software clock, *190*
command, *146*
compress/uncompress, *113, 121*
control files, *165*
copyleft, *10*
cpio, *53, 105, 113, 118*
    creating a cpio archive, *114*
    extracting files from a cpio archive, *118*
creating a new account, *73*
cron, *20, 89, 98, 150, 214, 227*

D

data transfer rate, *41*
database
    /usr/share/terminfo, *188*
datablock, *52*
date, *98, 190 - 192*
dd, *105, 121, 124*
defining terminals, *181*
depmod, *226*
    constructing the dependencies table , *225*
device identifier, *41*
df, *151, 154*
Digital UNIX, *32, 199*
directory
    /etc/rc.d, *28, 31*

/usr/news, *95*
disk space monitoring, *151*
dmesg, *19, 101*
du, *154*
dump, *53, 60, 105, 107, 111*
    backup, *108*

E

EBCDIC, *122*
epoch, *190*

F

fdisk, *68*
file
    $HOME/, *97*
    $HOME/.hushlogin, *177*
    .hushlogin, *95*
    .seq, *167*
    /boot, *18*
    /etc/dumpdates, *109*
    /etc/fstab, *20, 58 - 59, 69*
    /etc/gettydefs, *177, 179*
    /etc/group, *73*
    /etc/inittab, *21 - 23, 26, 177*
    /etc/issue, *180*
    /etc/login.defs, *96*
    /etc/motd, *95 - 96*
    /etc/nologin, *34*
    /etc/passwd, *73, 75, 78*
    /etc/powerstatus, *25*
    /etc/printcap, *162*
    /etc/psdatabase, *145*
    /etc/shadow, *73, 77 - 78*
    /etc/shells, *75*
    /etc/termcap, *181 - 182*
    /fastboot, *35*
    /lib/modules/x.y.z, *222*
    /proc, *134*
    /proc/filesystems, *43*
    /proc/kmsg, *19*
    /proc/partitions, *102*
    /usr/include/linux/acct.h, *207*

/usr/share/terminfo, *181*
/var/account/pacct, *199, 214*
/var/account/savacct, *213*
/var/account/usracct , *213*
/var/adm/wtmp, *202, 205*
/var/run/shutdown.pid, *35*
/var/run/utmp, *200, 202*
/vmuniz, *18*
fsck, *35*
inittab, *31*
linux2.y.z, *217*
lock, *165*
patch2.y.z+1, *217*
special file names, *100*
status, *166*
file identifier, *41*
file system
    Amiga FFS, *42*
    checking and repairing a file system: fsck, *65*
    creating a file system: mke2fs, *53*
    ext2fs, *53*
    FAT (File Allocation Table), *42*
    HPFS, *42*
    Minix, *42, 53*
    MS-DOS, *42, 53*
    structure of an ext2fs, *45*
    UFS, *42*
    unmounting a file system: umount, *61*
    Windows NT NTFS, *42*
    xfs, *53*
find, *114*
finger, *75*
flash ROM, *18*
floppy, *125*
free, *157*
FreeBSD, *42*
Free Software Foundation, *10*
fsck, *36, 60, 65 - 67*
fstype file systems, *152*
function
    acct(2), *199*
fuser, *61 - 62, 64*

G

getty, *20, 177*
getty_ps, *176*
GID, *75, 83, 85, 87, 208*
glibc-2, *14*
GNU, *10*
GNU cpio software suite, *127*
GNUacct6.3.2 software suite, *199*
groff, *210*
grotty, *210*
group descriptor, *46*
group management, *83*
    primary groups, *83*
    secondary groups, *83*
groupadd
    creating a group, *85*
groupdel, *88*
    deleting a group , *88*
groupmod, *86 - 87*
    modifying group characteristics, *86*
grpck, *86*
    checking the /etc/group file , *86*
GUID, *57*
gunzip, *218*
gzip/ungzip, *113, 121, 217*

H

halt, *35*
history of user sessions: last, *202*
HOST, *128*
HPUX, *119, 199*
HUSHLOGIN, *96*

I

IBM, *123*
IDE, *125*
    connector, *100*
    disk drive, *100*
inclusion
    dynamic, *220*
    static, *220*

infocmp, *183, 186, 188*
init, *19 - 20, 27, 137, 179*
initialization scripts, *28*
    Redhat, *28*
    Slackware, *31*
inode, *41, 51*
    table, *46*
    bitmap, *46*
insmod, *223*
installation, *10*
ISO9660, *42*
IPC (Inter Process Communication), *227*

J

JCPU, *136*

K

kernel
    compiling, *218*
kerneld, *227*
kill, *35, 139, 147*
killall, *147*
killall5, *147*
klogd, *20*
kmod, *227*
Ksh, *93*
kswapd, *145*

L

LANG environment variable, *191*
last, *198, 202 - 203, 205*
lastcomm, *198, 209*
lib5, *207*
lib6, *207*
libc, *13*
limiting user resources, *93*
line printer daemon: lpd, *161*
Linus Torvalds, *10*
Linux file system
    ext2fs, *43 - 44*
Linux single, *22*
listing the mounted file systems: /etc/mtab, *56*

listing the storage devices, *101*
loadable modules, *220*
    compiling/installing the loadable modules, *222*
    preparing the kernel, *221*
    using , *223*
lock, *165*
logging utilities, *20*
login, *90 - 91*, *142*
    configuring user connections, *90*
login name, *89*
login shell, *177*
lpc, *171*
    administrating the printing system, *170*
lpd, *20*, *161*, *173*
lpq, *169*
lpr, *168*
lprm, *170*
ls, *110*, *115*, *118*
lsmod, *224*
    listing loaded modules, *224*

M

mail system, *89*
make config, *221*
make modules, *222*
make modules_install, *222*
MBR, *18*
mgetty, *176*
Miquel van Smoorenburg, *22*
mkdosfs, *53*
mke2fs, *53*, *55*
mkfs.ext2, *53*
mkfs.minix, *53*
mkfs.xiafs, *53*
mkswap, *68*
mkxfs, *53*
modprobe, *226 - 228*
monitoring system activity:uptime, w, *135*
monitoring the memory and the CPU: vmstat, *148*
monitoring the swap: swapon, free, *157*
mount, *55 - 56*
    mounting a file system, *55*

mount point, *55*
mt, *127 - 128*
    handling tapes, *127*
multi-user mode, *22*

N

newgrp, *85*
news, *95*
NextStep, *42*
NFS, *20*
nice, *142*
NT, *42*

O

off, *179*
OS/2, *42*

P

passwd, *88*
PCPU, *136*
PID, *137, 139, 143*
POSIX, *12*
POSIX.1, *119*
POSIXLY_CORRECT, *151, 154*
POST, *18*
poweroff, *37*
PPID, *137*
principles of system administration, *15*
printcap, *164*
PRINTER, *168*
printer service configuration: /etc/printcap, *161*
printing command: lpr, *168*
process
    groups, *139*
    init, *200*
    login, *200*
    scheduling, *141*
    states, *139*
process accounting
    structure of process accounting records, *207*
process management, *137*
    spawning processes, *137*

process states
- ready for execution, *139*
- stopped, *140*
- waiting-interruptible, *139*
- waiting-uninterruptible, *140*
- zombie, *140*

processes
- identifying, *62*

procinfo, *150*
procps-1.01 software suite, *134*
ps, *144*, *146*
pstree, *138*
pwck, *78*

Q

QIC, *125*

R

RAID (Redundant Array of Independent Disks), *42*, *216*
reboot, *35*, *37*, *204*
rebuilding the kernel, *217*
RedHat, *21*, *28*, *36*, *69*, *191*, *225*
remote archiving and restoring, *130*
remote printing, *173*
renice, *142 - 143*
respawn, *177*, *179*
restore, *105*, *111*
- a local archive, *131*
- a remote archive on to your local site, *131*

restriction
- hard, *94*
- soft, *94*

rmmod, *228*
rpc, *20*
rsh, *130*
runlevels, *21 - 22*, *24*
- changing the runlevel, *27*
- finding out the current runlevel, *27*

S

sa, *198, 207, 211*
    using accounting information, *209*
SCO, *42*
script
    rc, *28 - 29*
    rc.local, *28 - 29*
    rc.sysinit, *28 - 29*
SCSI disk drive, *100, 125*
sendmail, *20*
SGID bit, *85*
Shadow software suite, *34, 85, 90, 91, 142*
shutdown, *34, 37, 48, 204*
SIGHUP signal, *27*
SIGINT signal, *25, 204*
SIGKILL signal, *34, 63, 140*
SIGPWR signal, *24*
SIGTERM signal, *34, 147, 209*
single user mode, *21*
    rebooting, *37*
Slackware, *28, 36, 69, 191, 225*
spool queue management: lpq, lprm, *169*
status, *166*
strftime, *98*
SUID, *57, 144*
SunOS, *32, 42, 199*
superblock, *46 - 47*
swap
    activating a swap area: swapon, *69*
    deactivating a swap area: swapoff, *70*
    setting up a swap area: mkswap, *68*
swap management, *68*
swapoff, *70*
swapon, *69, 157*
sync, *48, 66*
syslogd, *20*
system
    re-starting, *32*
    stopping, *32*

System V, *19, 21 - 22, 28, 44, 84 - 85, 119, 147, 160, 176, 181, 199*
sysvinit software suite, *22, 32*

T

TAPE environment variable, *112*
tape management, *125*
tar, *53, 105, 111, 113, 118, 127, 217*
tar versus cpio, *120*
tarfile, *111*
TCP/IP, *128*
telinit, *179*
TERM environment variable, *182*
termcap, *183*
termcap databases, *182*
terminal management daemons, *176*
terminfo databases, *183*
tic, *183, 187 - 188*
time zone management, *193*
toe, *184*
troff, *210*
tsch, *75*
tune2fs, *49*

U

UID values, *75, 80, 89, 208*
ulimit - ulimit -a, *93 - 94*
umount, *61*
Unix and Linux, *11*
Unix BSD, *42*
Unix System V, *42*
unloading a module: rmmod, *228*
updating the kernel source code, *217*
uptime, *135 - 136*
user information, *95*
useradd, *74, 79*
    creating a user account, *79*
userdel, *89*
    deleting an account, *89*
usermod, *87 - 88*
    modifying a user account , *88*

utilities
- archiving and restoring, *106*

V
vmlinuz, *18*
vmstat, *148, 150*

W
w, *136*
who, who am i, *198, 200 - 201*
Windows 95, *42*
Windows 98, *42*
Windows NT 4, *42*
write, *201*

Z
zdump, *193*